Tracking the Storm

Uncovering the Pattern to Great Crisis

Carl E. Creasman, Jr.

Published by:
Carl E. Creasman, Jr.
P.O. Box 217
Winter Park, FL 32790

www.carlcreasman.com

Printed in the United States of America

ISBN #: 978-0-9814638-2-7

Table of Contents

One

The Coming Turn

On September 13 1858, slave catchers under the authority of the 1850 Fugitive Slave Act kidnapped a young black man. The young man, John Price, was captured in the city of Oberlin, OH, north in the state, some 30 miles west of Cleveland. When news of the kidnapping reached Oberlin, home to one of the nation's first Colleges to admit African-Americans to study, over 40 members of the town raced to Wellington, OH where Price had been taken. After attempts to negotiate Price's freedom failed, the men stormed the hotel where Price was being held, rescued him and whisked him off to safety back in Oberlin.

Two days after Price was captured, in Jonesboro Illinois, Abraham Lincoln would continue his ongoing debates with Senator Stephen Douglas for that November's Senatorial election. Jonesboro was the 3rd of what would be 7 debates; the previous site of Freeport had produced Senator Douglas' position that would become known as the "Freeport Doctrine" which would be a broad support for the concept of "popular sovereignty." The Lincoln-Douglas debates would eventually end with Douglas holding his Senate seat, but would catapult Lincoln into the national conscious as a leading moderate voice in the growing tension about slavery.

Had you asked an average American about either event in the hot days of September, you would have gotten a blank stare or perhaps a shrug of the shoulders. While certainly many Americans were hearing more about national news than any other time in our short history at that point, the reaction by Ohioans to the Fugitive Slave Act would have been muted. Many Americans simply would not have even heard about the capture of Price, though later historians would consider this moment a critical one on the journey to the Civil War. By the same token, historians clearly see the

Lincoln-Douglas Debates as a major moment, both for the young Republican Party and Lincoln, on the road to the Civil War.

Certainly, the events of the previous 10 years since the conclusion of the Mexican-American War had been rife with dissention and violence, including fighting reaching the hallowed halls of Congress itself. Many citizens could feel as if the country was unraveling somewhat and clearly the political leaders' vitriol was as stark as it had been in anyone's memory. Where previously a spirit of compromise seemed to prevail among the leaders of the country, now it seemed as if there was a philosophical divide that was threatening the country.

What Americans were feeling was the turn towards a major crisis that would soon engulf the country in a military struggle to solve a philosophical question about government that was embedded with a moral dilemma about human rights and dignity. No one could have foreseen how these events would transpire, however, and that is the point that I want to focus on. Events come that seem somewhat innocent enough, yet become part of a larger story, a "Road to Great Crisis" that, if we look around us, can be seen in the events of our modern history.

The two events, the Oberlin-Wellington Rescue and the Lincoln-Douglas Debates, coming as they did in the early fall of 1858, did not seem to portend danger. In fact, many observers of the times would have missed the significance of these moments in general terms. The real dust-up had happened in 1855-56 during the "Bleeding Kansas" period. Between the end of 1856 and fall of 1858, active violence had ceased and concerned citizens assumed that the national problem was on the way to being solved. Or, that perhaps this was just a territorial issue in the West.

People assuming this would be wrong, as we now know. But even though the events of 1857 were monumental as well, especially the infamous Dred Scott Supreme Court case, those issues seemed to be the normal decisions and issues of the political realm. So, for the two years till John Price's capture, nothing "nation gripping" seemed to emerge.

What happens in events, though, is that things can and do become like dominoes impacting other things around it. Each year I have my students learn to discern "cause and effect" relationships between major events in history. They create something like a "Road to the Civil War" where they attempt to uncover what things transpired that took the country from the supposed high success of seeing Manifest Destiny supreme with the conclusion of the Mexican War to the scary reality of civil war. The war did not "just happen," but rather emerged due to a series of events. It is the fact that these events can seemingly have little connection but ultimately impact one another that I want my students to see. That is what I want you to see. Being able to discern patterns among events can help you prepare for your own future.

Though no one would have known, the Oberlin-Wellington Rescue would be part of the motivation for a native Ohioan, John Brown. In the fall of 1857, John Brown was working his way through the abolitionist New England area trying to raise support and funds. Brown had gone to Kansas to aid some of his sons who had moved there as part of the "free-soilers" effort to create a slave-free Kansas. That his sons had gone in that effort is not surprising since Brown had long been an ardent abolitionist. As a child, Brown's family had moved to Hudson, OH, which is located near Oberlin, and his father had even served as a financial supporter of the young Oberlin College effort in the 1830s. His father was even considered a "station master" in the growing "Underground Railroad," so while John Brown had little adult success in business, he had been raised "in a family that hated slavery in a town that hated slavery."

While in Kansas, Brown had been among the abolitionists who decided to "fight fire with fire." He was responsible for the deaths of 5 slave owners, partially in response to the Sack of Lawrence, an act of the "bleeding Kansas" period. He returned to raise funds not just to deal with Kansas, but with a larger dream in mind—raising an army of freed slaves. To do this, he proposed to capture the Federal arsenal at Harpers Ferry, VA. This city, some 350 miles southeast of Oberlin, would thus be connected to John Price via the actions of John Brown.

A year after the Oberlin-Wellington Rescue, John Brown would attack and seize the arsenal. He had an "army" of 21 men, including at least 3 men from Oberlin (two of them were "Rescuers" of Price). Brown's hoped-for army of runaway slaves never materialized and ultimately, his effort ended in failure. Or did it? Brown would be tried and convicted of treason against the state of Virginia and hung. His death galvanized both the north and the south.

For southerners, this was the proof that abolitionists, and probably anyone associated with abolitionists, would stop at nothing to change was Southerners thought was their natural right and way of life. Cities and counties all across the south would start arming militias and preparing to defend themselves, ultimately creating what would be the core of the Confederate army.

For northerners, the execution of Brown was more complicated. To abolitionists, this was proof that the South was not concerned about freeing the slaves and the worst nightmare could become true—slaves in the territories, perhaps extending the national life of slavery longer than anyone could imagine. However, for non-abolitionists northerners, the trial, set as treason against Virginia, raised the fear that Southerners were not interested in the long-term preservation of the nation as a whole, but only selfishly focused on their own state issues.

In any case, the road from Oberlin to Harpers Ferry was one that began in the shroud of obscurity and ended in the blinding light that the two sides of the country were entrenched in ways that could only end poorly. Brown was executed December 2, 1859 and wrote, "I, John Brown, am now quite certain that the crimes of this guilty land will never be purged away but with blood. I had, as I now think, vainly flattered myself that without very much bloodshed it might be done."

Eleven months later on November 6, 1860, the loser of the Illinois Senatorial election, Abraham Lincoln would be elected President. Six weeks later on December 20, 1860, South Carolina would secede from the Union and the Civil War Conflict was assured.

Two

The Pattern of History

So why do old events from the 1850s matter to us? The answer lies in a 500-year-old pattern that occurs throughout Anglo-American history. The pattern provides us with clues to what is going on around us, and clearly a lot is going on around us. Throughout history, observers of culture and history have noted that life seems to work in large-scale patterns. Obviously, various cultures and societies have their own unique aspects that bring trends and patterns to them somewhat differently than other places, but overall, it is clear that we humans seem to be in a loop.

"Why" is not totally clear. Is it because we are mere creatures of habit? Is it because we always fail to learn from the past, thus doomed to repeat? Is there something in the pattern that suggests a divine set-up? Regardless of the why, clearly one can see such patterns throughout history. Whether looking at something like the propensity for Americans to return often to electing war-heroes as President, or a nation like France going through repeated cycles (since the 1800s) of revolution, Republic and Empire, or even on the smaller stage of "the sins of the father" being seen in the life of the children, repeatable patterns are around us.

I was first introduced to this concept while studying history at Auburn University back in the 1980s. Various professors that I had, mostly European focused, had noted at different places the obvious fact of a repeating pattern—sometimes on a small scale, other times on longer views. It was at this time that I first read Arthur Schlesinger Jr.'s book *Cycles of American History*. In that work, he postulated a two-cycle swing in American history. Working off earlier writings, starting with his historian father, Schlesinger produced evidence that the USA consistently swung between periods of "public activity" and "private interest." He tied this flow to generations and their approach to events of the time. The idea that each generation would have attributes related to their parents, either similar or in reaction against, was not new to either Schlesinger.

A decade later in the '90s, I first read the book *Generations* by William Strauss and Neil Howe. In this powerful book, I was introduced to their take on the larger concept of patterns, generations, the circular saeculum (in usage from the ancient Romans, the saeculum was "a natural century" or the equivalent of a long human life), parenting and the rhythm of American history. As I read, and later enjoyed their second, more powerful book, *The Fourth Turning* (published in 1997), I immediately renewed my study of Schlesinger and the concept of historical cycles. This was the start of my interest in the patterns that lead into the 4th Turning, how consistent the pattern of crisis-awakening was, and the impact of societal parenting views on generations.

When I began teaching history at Valencia Community College in 2002, I started to dig deeper into the pattern that Howe and Strauss wrote about; things became even more apparent. Thus, between the reading of their works, my own private study and the teaching of history, I began to formulate a viewpoint that builds directly off of Howe and Strauss.

What I teach at Valencia are the larger survey type courses, which allows me to cover both American history and European (Western Civilization) history in broad swaths. Just as we know that flying higher in a commercial jet allows us to see the bigger picture of the landscape below, the survey course allows one to see the larger pattern of human life over its known existence.

That there is a predictable cycle of events in Anglo-American history, or has been over the past 500 years, is clearly observable, however the why behind it, as I said, is more obscure. The "why" is perhaps too hidden for anyone to uncover. I certainly won't ask you to just believe my take on it, but I do think you should accept the fact that a pattern exists. As Strauss & Howe said it, "What rhythm did Arnold Toynbee see rippling through the modern age of every civilization he studied? It's the unit of history the Etruscans discovered: the natural saeculum, history turning to the beat of a long human life."

So, what is the pattern? To start with, there exists four phases that occur generally through the generations. Each occurs roughly in 20-25 year periods, about the length of time for a specific generational group (like "The Boomers") to move from one life cycle stage to another. The concluding phase is what the ancients called "revolution," but Strauss and Howe make a convincing argument for "Crisis." The crisis comes at the end of the cycle, much like a winter metaphorically brings an "end" to the year. This "great crisis" occurs within the last period, the fourth turning.

If winter, a "crisis," brings the end, then the rebirth would be the first part of the cycle just as spring starts the year. This is the "High," the sense of survival through the hard days of the social crisis. Twenty years later as the generations move into the next life cycle phase, that feeling will ultimately lead to the second turning of Spiritual Awakening. Much like the joy of spring will lead to the exuberance of summer, there is a pinnacle much like the summer solstice. Yet, signals that the days will again grow short is similar to the emerging third phase, the "Unraveling," the period of social struggle and conflict that seems to portend harder days to come. And come it does, in the return of the Crisis, roughly 80-90 years after the start of the cycle.

Since the period of the Renaissance, Western history, within which the history of the USA is intertwined, that 4 phase cycle has moved. Within the saeculum, another clear two-fold pattern, working much like a helix, a two strand flow of history wrapping around one another, emerges. One the one hand, we have the strand of "Great Crisis," those events that become epic shaking, monumental and powerful enough to alter the society and culture that flows out of it. On the other hand, we have the strand of the "Great Spiritual Awakenings." Here, we see the human impulse for a search of meaning, for a connection with the Christian God (though later in the pattern, as we move into the 20th century, these Awakenings have included non-Christian impulses), the pinnacle of the joy of summer.

Along each strand of time, the Great Crisis or the Great Awakening occurs at roughly 80-year intervals. Connected to one another, each occurs 40 years apart from one another, thus society goes through a pattern by which they have a monumental crisis that wracks life, then 40 years later, a monumental spiritual awakening occurs as society takes a deep search for meaning.

Realize, as we look back, we should not seek to be locked into some search to discover 40 years to the day. You won't even be able to count 40 years exactly; some seasons are a few years less, a few years more. And, the experts have noticed that the flow of the individual phases seem to be compressing, growing smaller. Still, these large saeculum are close though; close enough to be seen. That is fact enough to direct us to try to make sense of what we know from before and then apply that to making better choices now.

Let's take a look at our current saeculum to help you see what I mean. Remember, the closer we are historically to an event, the harder it is for us to have the proper perspective relative to the veracity of what we think we see or know. With that in mind, loosely you can see that after World War 2, the mood of the country was "high" even with the Cold War swirling. Then came the assassination of President Kennedy and by 1966, something had changed, though it was not all "bad." This was the coming of the Second Turning, the Spiritual Awakening (the fourth in US history), what we typically call the "Consciousness Revolution." It is the first of the Awakenings to not be explicitly Christian. The spiritual explosion rolled into the Third Turning some 18-20 years later as Ronald Reagan was in his second term. Things seemed positive as President Reagan led the country to an economic comeback, leading to the financially explosive late '80s and Clinton's 90s. The hippies of the Awakening morphed into the Yuppies of the 90s. Yet, the "success" of the moment was tempered in many ways that reflected the typical Third Turning, the phase that Strauss and Howe call "Unraveling." Though we had won the cold war by 1989, it was soon clear that the world would not easily allow the USA to just police things. Economically, though Clinton's years seemed great, the reality was that a larger percentage of Americans were getting left behind in real income terms. Thus, as stated in the opening chapter of this book, the latter days of the '90s and first decade of the 21st century felt clearly to be unraveling, some 20 years since Reagan.

If you "do the math," it is clear that we are now in the early days of what Strauss and Howe call "the fourth turning." This is the moment when we find ourselves in winter. In fact, it is possible that the Great Crisis is among us, yet I think we are still a few years off from the peak, from the explosion. I think metaphorically, we find ourselves in 1858, a few years before Lincoln's election, before South Carolina withdraws, before Brown's raid. Or, it could be even earlier, maybe symbolically we are living in 1853, before "bleeding Kansas."

When Strauss and Howe wrote *The Fourth Turning,* they closed their book with some thoughts about the future. They published the book in 1997 and today, their words read staggeringly like proclamations from some Old Testament prophet. They thought of possible events that could provoke the Great Crisis: a financial crisis that leads to acts of secession as the President engages in acts to dominate the states; a global terrorist act involving airplanes or portable nuclear weapons; a crisis of federal political power as Congress and the President fight one another; a destructive pandemic; global crisis emerging in the former USSR, across Asia. That list sounds like it was written today.

My point in writing is not to rewrite the book Strauss and Howe already wrote; you should read their work directly. What I believe we can learn is what happened in the years leading up to the previous great crises. I think that within each of the previous 5 historical moments, there is yet another pattern, clues we can use to prepare. We are heading into the great crisis; if all of the previous ones held some observable patterns, or all seemed aimed at one clear point, we would do well to know what that is!

Three

The Great Crisis Upon Us

Could we possibly be in the last phase, the phase of a Great Crisis? Or, to use the season metaphor of Strauss and Howe, are we in the Winter of this current saeculum? I believe we clearly are. Not only have the predictions of Strauss and Howe come into focus, somewhat sharply in some of their thoughts, but a host of other events have begun to emerge that speak clearly of both unraveling (Third Phase) and coming crisis (Fourth Turning).

To anyone watching in 2010-2011, things in the USA certainly seem to be unraveling. In fact, the 15 years from 1990-2005 very clearly present a period of the country coming unhinged. We had the high period (generally) of the President Ronald Reagan years, though even that time was tumultuous, full of change and challenge domestically. Then the first Bush presidency never seemed to live up to the expectations, even with the successful Desert Storm War with Iraq and Kuwait. Bush's last year seemed beset with issues that then brought about Bill Clinton's successful 8 years. Yet, those years had a lot of personal greed and personal moral failures, not only for the President, but also for many others in America. Rather than some strong moral, conservative country that one could have assumed in 1986, by 1997-98, clearly things within the country were moving in different directions.

The election of George W. Bush did not actually assuage the fears of conservatives since he was a moderate like his father, a far cry from the Reagan conservative viewpoint. Worse, for Democrats, the various issues with the election itself convinced many that Bush had "stolen" the election. Then came 9/11 and everything in the country changed. From that time, it has seemed as if we have been rushing off a waterfall. But, we may instead only be rushing to the edge!

For the past decade then I have been watching closely for signs, look for any similarities to events like the Oberlin-Wellington Rescue or the Lincoln-Douglas Debates. At the same time, I have been listening to experts from multiple fields. Have you? If so, then you have probably noticed what I have—that many of these experts in disparate fields of focus (technology, biology, environment, space, finance, geo-politics, agriculture) are all talking about looming massive crisis that they believe will hit in the 2010-2020 decade.

The currently most famous example of this is the experts in the Ancient Mayan religion and culture. If you haven't heard, the Mayans understood time through a circular calendar or clock-type device. It was a very complex system that ultimately allowed them to incorporate various smaller cycles into what is known as "The Long Count." For some reason unknown to scholars, the Long Count stopped being counted in a way that concludes on December 21-23, 2012 (depending on which starting date a scholar uses, a choice of August 11-13, 3114 BC). Thus, to those who wish to see it as such, one can propose that the Mayan's predicted the end of the world (though there is no evidence that any such thing can be really concluded).

Adding to the hysteria is that December 21, 2012 is the Winter Solstice. That, of course, happens every year, but being the shortest day of the year seems to lead credence to the Mayan concern. And, for the trifecta, that is also the date that the earth, sun and the other planets of the solar system will align (either together or even with the "center of the universe"). This supposedly will either flip our magnetic poles or pull the earth out of orbit. Of course, modern scientist are working tirelessly to debunk any concern over these issues (I could also mention the mysterious, mystical planet of Nibiru that, while undiscovered, is actually on a collision course with Earth, but we'll leave that for another day), yet the sheer concept of the potential "end of the world" has motivated Hollywood to strike while they can with a new series of disaster movies such as *2012, The Road,* or *The Book of Eli.*

Still, the concept of the Mayan calendar strikes home at the point that I am trying to make. The decade of 2010-2020 is predicted to be horrible in a variety of ways. In no specific order, experts have predicted various world changes that, according to your own viewpoint, could be catastrophic. Staying in the stars, scientists who are experts on the sun have predicted a horrific decade of solar flares and issues with the sun. Geo-political analysts have suggested the China will invade Taiwan, North Korea will launch a nuclear attack at either South Korea or Japan, and that Russia will return to communism, perhaps attempting to reclaim her lost "States" like the Ukraine or Uzbekistan. Turkey at war with a new Kurdistan, Greece fighting to conquer a new Macedonia, Serbia battling Kosovo over independence---these are just a few of the regional explosions that are predicted. Certainly the recent revolutionary movements in Egypt, Yemen, Libya, Tunisia, Iran and Saudi Arabia

Military strife is not missing in North America as experts have predicted the coming of a new nation, combining Mexico, USA and Canada into one massive state. Yet, at the same time, since the middle Bush-presidency years, there have been more than 20 U.S. states with an active secessionist movement. The recent decision by Congress and President Obama relative to health care have pushed more than a dozen states preparing to sue the national government over the decision. Are these echoes of the South Carolina call for a General Convention over secession in December 1860?

Financially, as I write this in 2011, we already know of the economic disaster; yet many financial experts predict that this is the start of disaster, not the end. The same happened in 1932 when things got worse economically compared to 1930, even though the government had taken various steps to "fix things" since the start of the Great Depression. Some reports are that real wages are going to stay flat for at least another decade. Other experts are now saying that the average American family's economic buying power has actually been in decline since the early 1990s. In November 2010, the US Department of Labor reported the national unemployment rate at 9.3%, however many states and metro cities are far over 10%. And, most experts believe that the rate is far below the actual number, which some declare is about 20% nationally, and maybe close to 30% in our major cities. Early in 2009, I heard a report that quoted leading CEOs stating that perhaps the best case scenario for what they saw in the national economy was "a full reset," where prices and incomes plummeted down to real levels that accurately reflected real values. Necessary perhaps, but dreadful to contemplate, and that was their "best case scenario" for the country.

At the same time, other financial gurus have predicted the end of cash, the end of the penny and the beginning of people only needing to use their cell phones to make purchases. This move towards digital money is coming, of course, at the same time as more Americans slide deeper and deeper into debt. Almost 40% of the country owes over $10,000 in unsecured debt (that means not including their house or car loans). Over two million people owe more than $40,000.

Meanwhile, the national government is so far in debt that some geopolitical experts have predicted that China may call in our loans, though other scholars doubt that. Still, what if China asks for payment in the form of, say, Hawaii or Alaska? Even if there is no "arm twisting" to hype up the international crisis level, owing China over $800 billion (we also own Japan over $700 billion) is not a great place to be heading into the next decade. There is a real possibility of the USA simply not being able to pay its normal expenses to run the country (services, welfare, new health care, etc...), let alone any costs to foreign countries.

Obviously anyone with two ears knows all about the supposedly critical state of nature. Al Gore has made a new career for himself with his popular slideshow about global warming, and though other scientists disagree with what exactly is going on, experts predict massive "gloom and doom" situations that could begin in this next decade. Even average people living on the shores of the US report on the rising ocean levels. Other experts point to a growing critical shortage of water, often due to a US determination to create green spaces out of arid surroundings.

Other science "issues" are looming including studies that show the sun's solar radiation is actually decreasing, while other studies indicate that the earth's spin has been slowly speeding up since 1999. Few have missed the seeming increase in killer hurricanes, earthquakes, tsunami's and natural storms in general. While the knowledge of these events could only be the impact of a

24/7 news cycle, many scientists posit their happenings as more evidence that something is horribly wrong with earth and that impending disaster should hit this decade.

In the area of medical science and agrarian science, we are starting to figure out that all of the efforts in the 1950s-70s to eradicate diseases have only served to make the diseases mad. Back in full force are old favorites like polio, measles, rubella and mumps with adaptations made by the disease to make their punch more powerful. Many medical experts are predicting a nightmare pandemic to hit sometime in the next 10 years, with prediction of swine flu, avian flu, influenza and for some conspiracy experts, smallpox (considered to be the one disease that actually has been eradicated by science).

It's not just human diseases either; recently, agrarian experts discovered an outbreak of a return of stem rust, a deadly disease for wheat. Considered banished by science in 1970, it is now back, emerging from Africa. And it has returned angry! The disease is able to leap unpredictably long-range due to global travel and trade; worse, it is showing the ability to mutate meeting all new attempts by science to destroy it. Not a comic-book writer's new attempt at a super-villain, this disease could bring worldwide famine, or at least famine to China and India and the rest of Asia. Wheat provides a third of our calories worldwide. Even if famine does not come, fragile governments in countries on the path from Africa to China could ill afford or deal with such a crisis; ask the French of the 1780s-90s. And if the disease reached the USA where 40 million acres (our third most valuable crop) is vulnerable, the financial cost alone would be in the billions.

Maybe more troubling, and certainly factual, is that our bumblebee population has declined by up to 90% over the past two decades. That impacts you and me because the bumblebee plays a critical role in pollination throughout the food cycle. It has great impact on various foods like tomatoes, greenhouse vegetables and fruits. Perhaps more scary is that, like with the stem rust, the experts have no clue what caused this nor how to stop it.

Heard enough? How about this one? It is clear that with the explosion of Android, the iPhone and the new iPad, mobile computing (what one expert called "very personal computing"), there is a rising hue and cry for an even more open democracy; or, failing that (or in lieu of that for some), the end of nations and the start of one happy world. While the spread of information through open access should be a concept to celebrate, many of our founders would be horrified to hear many leaders and experts proposing the US move closer to a "more open Democracy," thus further away from the Founders creation of a Republic. Madison perhaps said it best that democracies have "ever been spectacles of turbulence and contention; have ever been found incompatible with personal security or the rights of property; and have in general been as short in their lives as they have been violent in their deaths." If you look around the globe, or just around the USA, it is easy to see that Madison was right, at least on the concept that Democracies are incompatible with property rights. The idea that moving to a true Democracy would lead the USA towards a violent death is perhaps debatable, but clearly we can see from elections of the past 80 years that we indeed have become a "spectacle of turbulence and contention."

The new technology, often trumpeted, and clearly nothing that we will ever be rid of (nor should we be), is also predicted to change education, media and entertainment. While those changes can hardly compare with the sun running out of light or the return of a killer super-virus that causes a worldwide famine, the concept of "always on, always connected" in a twitter-facebook-whatevernext society bodes ill on many fronts. Psychologists and educational experts are already concerned about the impact of so much media; children in the US are now spending over 7 hours a day with media (watching and creating), yet in a science-fiction styled concept, they are actually getting 11 hours of content in those 7+ hours. Scientists who focus on the study of the brain, as well as behavioral scholars, are now stating openly that our brains are changing, that we are losing the ability for critical thinking, due to the technology of the past decade.

Nutritionists take their concern in another direction, especially for the USA. Not only are children absorbing 11 hours or more of media, in our ever-loving quest for "things to watch," obesity has exploded. In the past 15 years, Americans have grown in weight to the point that every state but Colorado has 20%+ of their population obese. According to some surveys, the full population is close to a 30% rate of obesity.   Over 20% of US children are overweight or at high risk of adult obesity with the rate climbing.   One recent study determined that by 2015, 75% of Americans would be overweight or obese.

Including TV, Americans are getting over 60 hours of unduplicated media content, which largely means sitting and doing nothing.   Again, while this may pale compared to the world flooding due to melting ice caps, if this alone was the only crisis to hit in the 2010-2020 decade, it would easily exceed the financial cost of the civil war.   In today's dollars, the Civil War of 1861-1865 would have cost between $4 and 7 billion dollars (by comparison, World War 2 cost over $3 trillion and the Iraq war has cost over $900 billion).   Our obesity cost is over $140 billion a year, so for a 4-year effort the cost exceeds $560 billion, not a small issue for the society.

Whew—this is exhausting and scary reading, huh? See what I meant when I told you a great crisis was coming? If any of these scholars and experts is correct, the decade of 2010-2020 will be the most explosive known in about a century. I know for many of you intelligent readers, you may be leaping to defend our coming decade by proclaiming the equivalent of "so's your mother."   Or, more politely, the concept that every decade, every period of time has its own crisis, own issues, is presented as reason why we should not necessarily worry.   In general terms, I agree with that concept; each period of time does indeed have its own wars, economic crisis and scientific concerns.

My point, however, isn't some alarmists hysteria about any one of these things, but to reiterate that the experts in these disparate fields ALL point to this decade of 2010-2020 as the period of reckoning. This evidence of looming crisis for the USA (and the Western society in general) corresponds with the historical pattern. Winter is indeed upon us.

So, what is this pattern?

Four

Crisis Phase Overview

So, "let's do the math" backwards to see the previous Great Crisis as they exist from the perspective of Western Civilization. Of course, I realize that the USA is, today, the most ethnically diverse country on the planet, and thus most of our citizens are not "Anglo-Saxon." Yet, our connection in political theory, history and organization still has its roots in the experience of Europe, and more specifically England. Thus, while we could trace backwards towards events in Europe, we will limit ourselves to the cycles, the saeculums that are connected to the USA.

Before we dig too deep, it is important to note some key ideas. To start with, the fourth turning, that last period in the saeculum, is the same 20 years (roughly) of the other turnings or periods. Yet, the full explosion of the event is never that long. There is, within each fourth turning of our history, a moment when the "Great Crisis" explodes.

It is also important to realize that we must maintain some flexibility in determining these "phases." While history gives us a good grasp on when society made the turn from one period to the next, it is not as if one day the newspapers announced "today we start the fourth turning." Historians will not fully agree on when to even decide when a major event started. As an example, certainly we know that the firing on Fort Sumter is typically shown as the "start to the civil war," but any student of history knows that such a declaration is too simple. So, when did the civil war start? With the secession of South Carolina? Virginia, 5 months later? Lincoln's election? Certainly a date like December 7, 1941 rings with a certainty, but even in that instance, the USA was clearly involved with World War 2 before that fateful day

In the end, I have assigned dates to the phases that I think are accurate, as you can see from the following chart, but know that I do so recognizing that other historians might disagree at certain points. If you read Strauss and Howe's books, you'll quickly see that they do differ on some dates, usually by a few years. In the chart, you can see is that I have assigned the start of the actual Fourth period of crisis, but within each crisis period, we will discuss that the "Great Crisis" occurs at specific points. For both the Crisis and the Awakening, I list a "high point year" that gives us some sense that the critical event was moving finally towards its own conclusion.

	High	Awakening	High Point Year	Unraveling	Crisis 4th Turning	High Point Year
Reformation Age 1487 – 1594 (107 years)	Tudor Renaissance	Protestant Reformation 1517-1542	1529-30 Reformation Parliament Augsburg Confession	Wars of Religion	Wars of Philip II Spanish Armada 1569-1594	1588
Colonial Age 1594 – 1702 (108 years)	England Rising	Puritan Awakening 1621-1649	1640 (90 years to previous high point)	Restoration of Monarchy	Glorious Revolution 1675-1702	1688 (100 years to previous high point)
Revolution Age 1702-1788 (86 years)	Rise of English Colonial Empire	Great Awakening 1727-1746	1741 (101 years to previous high point)	French & Indian War	American Revolution 1765-1788	1780 (92 years to previous high point)
Civil War Age 1788-1868 (80 years)	Jeffersonian America	Second Great Awakening 1822-1844	1831 (90 yrs to previous high point)	Rise of Sectionalism & Division	Civil War 1855-1868	1863 (83 years to previous high point)
Great Power Age 1868-1948 (80 years)	Gilded Age	Third Great Awakening 1890-1908	1906 (75 yrs to previous high point)	WW 1 & Progressive Movement	Great Depression & World War 2 1929-1948	1943 (80 years to previous high point)

As you can see, the last great crisis of our country, all historians agree, was the Great Depression and World War 2 experience. Erupting in the 1930s, both the economic event and the subsequent war engulfed the country, and indeed the world. If we start in 1932, the year both Adolf Hitler and Franklin Delano Roosevelt were elected to lead their respective countries, we find ourselves 79 years to 2011.

If you subtract 77 years from the election year of 1932, you find yourself at 1855, three short years before the Oberlin-Wellington Rescue that we already spoke of. This would be the time of the upheaval connected to "bleeding Kansas," when the actual fighting of the soon-to-be civil war started in the west of the nation. The Civil War crisis racked the nation for 5 long years and then the Reconstruction that came after did not really set things right.

The coming crisis caused by the governmental decision to allow popular sovereignty in the territories of Kansas and Nebraska would have been familiar to the citizens of Boston 90 years before in 1765. The time of the Stamp Act would provoke those patriots, as well as other Americans all along the Eastern seaboard, to ALSO undertake violent acts of opposition to their government.

The attempt to oppose the British Monarch of 1765 would have been applauded by those brave men who were wrestling with the impact of the Test Act in 1675, some 90 years before the Stamp Act crisis. At the same time, the colonists in North America were starting one of the bloodiest wars in North America, Metacom's War or King Philip's War. Half of the English cities in New England were attacked while over 15% of the involved Native Americans would lose their lives.

These four crisis periods are the focus where we shall see a clear pattern of events. We must learn from these as we head into the 5th, possibly the last, of these cycles. Here they are in list form with the years for the overall phase as well as the "Great Crisis" event:

4th Turning		Great Crisis years
Glorious Revolution	1675-1702	1687-1690
American Revolution	1765-1788	1776-1781
American Civil War	1855-1868	1861-1865
Depression/WW2	1929-1948	1941-1945

"Doing the math" on the great crisis moments provides even more interesting findings. From Pearl Harbor back to Ft. Sumter is exactly 80 years (1941-1961). From Ft. Sumter back to the signing of the Declaration of Independence is 85 years. Subtract another 87 years and we arrive at the signing of the English Declaration of Rights (often called the "English Bill of Rights) associated with the Glorious Revolution. So, what about going forward? If we had 80 years from 1941 we reach 2021. Add the 85 years and we get to 2026.

Again, keep in mind that many experts have noticed that time has seemed to be compacting. Perhaps we should only add 75 years—that would have us arrive at 2016. Remember, we are talking about the actual "Great Crisis" at this point, the explosion within the fourth season, the fourth turning.

In the subsequent chapters, then, we will unpack each of these periods, looking to see if common attributes from the "Road to Crisis" can be uncovered. The road into the actual Great Crisis typically begins before the 4th Turning even occurs, during the Unraveling. We'll see some unique aspects to each, but I believe you will also see that each period has some commonalities. It is these events that should be our clue as we look at our own time.

Moreover, there is another aspect that should grab our attention. Each of these periods has led to one clear concept— overthrow or change of government. Strauss and Howe described the crisis as "when events trigger an upheaval in public life" and "struggles and sacrifices in an era of survival."

In each of the above events, there was no consensus among the participants with the possible exception of World War 2. The country and citizens were split, often philosophically, as to what course to take. The events have the feeling of a civil war, a fight within the society. Efforts during those periods were clearly being made to change the direction of government, even to the point of a complete overthrow of government.

Both the Glorious Revolution and the American Revolution did precisely that—overthrew the government making lasting, historical changes to the philosophy of politics. The third saeculum led to the US Civil War, which was an attempt to leave the government and establish a new country, just as their countrymen had done 85 years before. The union of northern states was successful at stopping that attempt, but at a cost. Though not clearly seen at the time, the style and power of the US government was changed. Lincoln's actions during the war clearly stepped outside the bounds of the Constitution and embarked a new era of a powerful central government. The Founders of Washington, Jefferson and Adams would have been horrified to see the government that Lincoln had created to save the Union.

The power of the new government would be seen in greater light within 40 years during the Progressive period and then completely unmasked by the actions of FDR. Certainly the World War 2 fourth turning can be characterized as the USA fighting to protect "democratic government" from the excesses of totalitarian governments like Italy and Germany. Yet, domestically, much like Lincoln, to achieve "victory" against the Axis and against the Depression, FDR leapt far beyond the Constitution, even to the point of threatening to pack the Supreme Court with men who would support his actions.

So, while technically, neither the Civil War nor World War 2 crises actually produced an overthrow of the United States' government, the direction of the country was radically changed with the outcome. In both cases, as Strauss and Howe predict with any fourth turning, the subsequent years are experienced as a "new civic order" which is perceived by the supporters as a "High." Of course, if you asked the Loyalists of the American Revolution period or the royalists who supported the monarchy of James II, they would not see that time as a "high," certainly not enjoyable.

In the end, the old saw that "the victors write the history" holds mostly true here. Certainly, "to the victors go the spoils," including determining how the government will act, what its powers will be, and what the rights and liberties of the citizens will be. As we head into the gale-force winds of our own fourth turning, we should be well aware what is at stake. Now do you see why the fact that over 20 states have active secession movements, both under President Bush and now, President Obama, should concern you?

Is there a pattern? Are there clues we need to be watching for? Let's take a short trip back through history to try and unpack what we can glean from these previous Great Crisis moments.

Five

The Glorious Revolution

The Glorious Revolution period came at the end of a tumultuous century in England. Exciting events like the founding of 3 colonies in the New World had been paired with religious and political turmoil at home. The middle of the century had seen England's Civil War erupt between Parliament and the Monarch, Charles I. Subsequent decades had had an attempt of a return to normalcy during the Restoration, but the third phase of unraveling held true. Overseas, the colonies, now bolstered with the conquest of land between Virginia and New England, led by the dashing Duke of York, took on a more independent role as the crown dealt with issues at home.

In 1685, Charles II, the son of the dethroned and decapitated Charles I, had died suddenly through an accident while horseback riding. Charles II had struggled mightily during the unraveling years of the "Restoration" to maintain control, keep his independence and corral the antagonistic Parliament. By the same token, members of Parliament fought to grasp full control of the English system of government. Though they had requested Charles return to assume the monarchy (after it became clear that Parliament was not fully capable of directing the country), the legislative voice of the country was determined to control the monarchy.

At the same time, the religious struggles between the Catholics, the Anglicans and the more strident Puritans (Anglicans who were determined to purify the Anglican Church from any hint of Catholicism, hence the nickname), had intensified. So, the concern within the country wasn't limited to how well Charles governed, but also included the religious choices, especially those of his brother James. Charles had not had any children, so it looked as if the crown would transition to James. Parliament had taken overt actions to control this fact, but now, with the death of Charles, James would become James II.

Two years later, with war erupting in the colonies, leaders in Parliament began to have discussions with Protestant William of Orange from The Netherlands. When James II announced his new wife was pregnant, the concerns of Parliament grew, especially the Puritan aspect. Once the birth occurred June 10th to a son, James Francis Edward, the leaders knew they had to move now or never, so on June 30th, they sent an invitation to William to invade their country, promising their support.

The successful invasion took place November 5th 1688 with the King's supporters and his army mostly sitting this one out. The Navy, led by closer allies, wanted to engage the Dutch navy, but "a Protestant Wind" prohibited the Royal Navy from sallying forth in battle. Once William had landed, it was clear that no one was going to really challenge him and King James II had actually fled the country. By the new year of 1689, the leaders of Parliament had written the Declaration of Rights that both William and Mary, as joint-monarchs, would happily sign. In December 1689, that document was made, by an Act of Parliament, the English Bill of Rights.

Had Charles II or James II been a bit more attentive, they may have "seen this coming." Or not, but we have the luxury of time perspective to be able to now see the clear steps of the "Road to Revolution." The success of the Restoration of 1660 was accompanied with parades, parties and general celebration. Five years later, the restored Stuart king and his brother would become embroiled in the ongoing geopolitical struggle on the Continent brought on by France's brilliant king, Louis XIV.

Though England had survived the previous Great Crisis in the 1580s Spanish Armada, she was not the dominant power of Europe yet. In fact, that next 100 years were something of a national competition between England and France that would continue into the next century. By the 1670s, it seemed that France was clearly the winner. Louis XIV had taken about 20 years to consolidate his control on the country and then in 1667 embarked on what would be the first of 4 major wars to expand the national borders. The 1667 war had his armies marching towards the Low Countries, land that had belonged to Spain since before the 1400s. However, in the late 1500s, northern provinces owned by Spain had successfully become independent as The Netherlands.

When France began to move towards The Netherlands, this opened the door for Charles II to provide his new reign with glory of its own. He had spent the long years of exile in the court of Louis XIV, so to some degree, it was right that he saw a chance to help his benefactor, but at the same time, he was aware that the young Dutch nation was becoming a seafaring rival of England. In the 1620s, the Dutch had successfully planted a colony in the New World north of England's land in the Chesapeake region. When the Pilgrims, and then later, the Puritans landed north of what was then called New Netherlands, conflict was probable. The Dutch certainly planned for it by building Fort Amsterdam, protection for what would be called New Amsterdam, on the island of Manhattan. By the 1667, Charles was eager to conquer this land and connect the English colonies, thus helping Louis XIV was convenient.

At home, though things were starting to grow tense. In 1665, the dreaded Plague returned to England and London was severely hit. One year later, the London fire would destroy most of London, leaving thousands homeless. Charles, of course, set about to rebuild the city, but largely, the crown and country were in debt by millions of dollars. Parliament leaders would begin to blame this on Edward Hyde, the Earl of Clarendon and in 1667, would effectively remove him from power.

This was not the only evidence of Parliament's determination to remain in control, even in the Restoration. In this same period, they set up the Committee of Public Accounts to account for how the King spent money. Fairly normal by our standards, at the time, it was incredible for the people to believe that they could tell the King how to spend the money. Since Charles was essentially broke, he looked again to Louis XIV for help. This seemed to many citizens that Charles was making decisions that would begin to get into the topic of religion, especially when the Catholic Louis XIV demanded that Charles publically concert, which he did in 1670.

Over the next decade, there would be a series of acts and decisions by the King and the Parliament that would increase the turmoil. In 1670, the King issued a Declaration of Indulgence, which he said was meant to provide more liberty for Protestant non-conformists. Leaders in Parliament and Puritans in general saw this as opening the door for Catholics to assert renewed power in England, thus the following year Parliament passed the Test Act which would deny the right of holding office to anyone but an Anglican. This argument over religion would become synonymous for a struggle over power; who could control leadership in England. For those keeping score at home, this was the same fight that had led to the English Civil War in 1642, the same conflict that had gotten Charles' father beheaded.

While Charles was struggling to maintain control, dodge alleged plots on his life (Popish Plot of 1678, Rye House Plot of 1683), and keep international balance with France, his brother James was becoming more of an issue. James had openly declared himself a Catholic in 1672 and then, the following year, took for his second wife Maria of Modena, a faithful Catholic princess. While this bothered many, it was overlooked in the hopes that King Charles would have a son and raise him as a Protestant. Those hopes died with the King in the horseback riding accident in February 1685.

Now events began to move more quickly, something we will note with all of the Great Crises. The seemingly unrelated horseback riding event prompted leaders in Parliament to meet secretly seeking possible actions they could take due to the sudden death of Charles. Meanwhile, initially, James II was received well as the new King. His stock also rose at first during two military invasions, first from Scotland and then from the illegitimate son of the now-dead king. The Monmouth Rebellion was a short-lived uprising that King James II handled well. . .until his crackdown on Monmouth's peasant supporters after the rebellion led to over 400 executions. For some, this had the look of a Catholic King lashing out in religious fervor against a Protestant uprising.

While James may not have meant it that way, he did present plans that could be interpreted as trying to turn England back to Catholicism. He demanded the repeal of the Test Act and he also issued a Declaration of Indulgence. His issuance was an attempt to build a political alliance between Catholics and Non-conformists. It was met coolly. Later, when he issued a second Declaration that he demanded to be read in every church, seven Anglican bishops refused. They were jailed in June 1688.

Through the three-year reign, tensions were high, but most in Parliament were content to wait James out. He was in his mid-50s and his two daughters of his first marriage were Protestant. There seemed no reason to rashly end up in yet another Civil War, as their ancestors had done 40 years before. Now, in June, Parliamentary leaders faced their worst fear—a royal son was born, a future King who would be raised Catholic. Now they had to act.

On June 30, 1688, leaders of Parliament sent an invitation to William of Orange from the Netherlands, the husband of the eldest daughter of James II, Mary, to come to their aid. These men were determined to pull off an act of high treason only slightly moderated because Mary was indeed the daughter of James. They tried build support for this act of treason by openly declaring that the young baby, named James, was not really a royal child but merely a "water pan baby" brought in from a servant girl, or worse, the baby of a prostitute. There is no evidence of any such tampering, but the charge stuck, probably because of how James II acted during the invasion.

Yet, nonetheless, the leaders had reached their breaking point and now, there was no going back. Regardless of what happened next, they had taken the critical act that would, in effect, be lighting the dynamite. From the middle 1660s to this moment, choices had been made, steps had been determined that moved slowly, but surely, towards this explosion. The next year would be revolutionary and would open the door on more extreme change in England, both politically and militarily. A new round of warfare would open that would impact the next major crisis, a series of wars that would end with England as the dominant power in 1763, but teetering in debt and with a new revolution brewing an ocean away.

Six

The American Revolution

In the spring of 1754, a young twenty-two year old led a small group of 150 Virginians towards a critical river confluence northwest of the colony. The young man, George Washington, had spent the previous year surveying the area for the colonies' governor, Robert Dinwiddie. The fact that the land laid directly west of William Penn's colony did not dissuade the Virginians who had long seen most of North American as merely an extension of their original colony created in the late 1500s, and successfully founded at Jamestown in 1607.

Washington and his few soldiers would soon find themselves embroiled in an international affair with French soldiers, complicated by Native Americans who were clearly "playing both sides" in a desperate attempt to hold onto their lands. The clash consisted of fighting in late May through early July before the French prevailed and forced Washington to retreat on July 4th, 1754.

These were the first shots of what would be known in Europe as the Seven Years War, though more famously in the United States as the French and Indian War. The fighting near current day Pittsburgh would resume the next year when the British High Command would actually send troops to the New World. The appearance of British regulars in North America would alter the relationship between the colonies and the mother country and ultimately propel events in North America that would end up with another critical event happening on a different July 4th, 22 years later in 1776.

The years between the Glorious Revolution and the French and Indian war had been good ones in the colonies. Population had quintupled by 1750 from 250,000 to 1.25 million in only 50 years. Economically, the country was developing well, with the major cities easily among the richest in the British lands (India, Caribbean, Africa, North America). There had been some conflict in North America relative to the ongoing geopolitical rivalry between England and France, but most of that had been limited to New England.

Yet, in England, the wars had taken their toll. The aging king, George II, was 71 when Washington had stumbled into crisis near the Ohio River. There had been a new invasion of Scotland by the descendant of James II which was put down in 1746 while the country found itself drawn into political issues and war from central Europe. There, tense relationships between Prussia and Austria would drag both France and England again into battle. The War of Austrian Succession ended with the Treaty of Aix-la-Chapelle in 1748, thus with only six years of breathing space till conflict erupted in North America.

The colonies had actually contributed to the outbreak of war in the 1740s due to British shipping and some degree of piracy. England was trying to break Spain's monopoly on trade from the New World using any means necessary. When one of England's captains, Robert Jenkins, was captured and then promptly had his ear cut off for good measure, England responded with war. This fighting had led to action in England's youngest colony, Georgia and an invasion of Spanish Florida to attempt capture of St. Augustine.

When George II died in 1760, he was exhausted from war, just as the nation was. His grandson, George III took the throne at the age of 22, four years younger than the American George. King George III was determined to get the country out of war and hopefully move her onto solid footing economically. To do that, he would turn to a series of political leaders who could seemingly do nothing right in their attempt to "fix the economy." George in many ways was caught in the difficult political realities created by the Glorious Revolution.

That revolution had determined, once and for all, that Parliament would dominate the governance of England. William, Mary, Anne and then her cousin George of Hanover all seemed happy enough with the situation. George II though had chaffed some under the political leadership of Robert Walpole, England's first Prime Minister. Walpole had guided George I easily enough, mostly because the King could not speak any English.

By the time of George III, though German in ancestry, the King was every bit an Englishman, and yet schooled in the concept of kingly leadership. While he certainly never thought of re-establishing an absolute monarchy, he clearly believed the Monarchy should be at the center of decisions. The fact that he was operating within a vicious political game in the House of Commons between the Whigs and the Tories should make the Road to the American Revolution more clear to modern-day Americans who watch our own leaders struggle. When we see direction in the country, what is best for us, somehow used as a political weapon between the two major parties, we can sense that it is hard for any leader to truly provide healthy leadership.

George contributed to his own troubles when he replaced the popular Whig leader, William Pitt, in the king's efforts to get the country out of war. Thereafter, the Whigs would often make political hay at the King's expense, no matter what was really going on in the colonies. And, it was in the colonies that the real conflict would emerge.

In June of 1754, just one month before Washington would ignobly retreat back to Virginia, a collection of leaders from seven of the colonies met in Albany, NY. After five decades of some warfare relative to France, these leaders thought they should help determine how to defend themselves. They would ultimately propose a variation of unity that is similar to the Commonwealth system employed by England in the 1800s. Ben Franklin put forth an idea of a colonial parliament with a leader appointed by the King (a variation of the Prime Minister); it never really got off the ground in the colonies. At that point, the majority of colonists saw no reason for such a radical suggestion. There is no evidence that the King or Parliament would have accepted the idea.

As the conflict came to a successful end in 1763, the colonists were eager to return to a "business as usual" model. However, the new king's ministers, led by Prime Minister George Grenville, had determined that the easiest way to alleviate the debt crisis was to raise taxes in the colonies. Up to that point, the colonies paid about 1/50th of the tax compared to their fellow citizens in England. Worse, with the decision to send troops to North America, England now had to come up with more money to support protecting the colonies. For many in England, it seemed obvious that the colonies should pay for their own protection; wouldn't that be what any good citizen would do? No one thought to actually ask the colonies.

Since the tension that demanded troops lay with the Native Americans, Grenville started actions by making a proclamation that prohibited any territorial advance over the Appalachian Mountains. This was a reasonable request, yet it cut directly against how the colonists viewed their own lives. For even the colonists with long established roots in the main American cities, the concept of "Going west" to build a new life was part of their DNA. The King's decision to limit their expansion struck most Americans as infringing on their freedom to go where they wished.

However, it was the economic decisions of Grenville that got the strongest reaction. A series of new laws, "acts" as they were known, were passed in 1764 and '65, all aimed at raising taxes to deal with the monetary crisis of the country. Grenville even took the liberal position of asking the Colonial Representatives to check off on these decisions, particularly his most far-reaching act, the Stamp Act of 1765. With their representatives on board, Grenville assumed logically that the colonies would accept these measures. They might have, had it not been for a few angry firebrands living in Virginia and Massachusetts.

In Boston, 43-year-old lawyer Samuel Adams, the son of a Bostonian who had lost a fortune in a British banking collapse, saw these efforts by Grenville in a very different light. Through 1763-65, Adams would emerge as a leading voice opposing the Acts by Parliament, stating openly that the colonists could not be taxed since there was no representation in Parliament. This was the start of a disagreement about the correct interpretation of the rules of the British government. Note, England had no official Constitution, just a loose collection of Acts, such as the English Bill of Rights, that collectively was seen as the governing documents. Men like Adams took a radically different view of the role of Parliament.

Soon, Adams joined others who decided to take their frustration to the streets. These "thug gangs" would use violence and force to terrorize their neighbors who dared to support the government. At the same time, representatives from nine colonies would meet in New York City in the Stamp Act Congress. This "legal opposition" was the counter-weight against the "street violent opposition" of groups like the Liberty Boys, the Loyal Nine and the Sons of Liberty. Men like John Adams, a second cousin of Sam Adams, had already written openly against the actions of the crown, though he was strongly against all forms of violent protest such as burning down houses or the infamous "tar and feathering."

The opposition soon provided Grenville's opponents in Parliament their chance to strike at him, and through him, the King. Taking the colonial opposition as their rallying point, the Whigs demanded a repeal (though the majority of them had voted for the Act when it was first passed). Eventually, Ben Franklin was called to give an account for the actions of the colonists. Franklin, the representative of Pennsylvania, had also supported the Act proposed by Grenville, but as news of the opposition (which included the home of his personal friend being burned down by an angry mob) reached him, he acted like a skillful politician and shifted gears. During the trial, while he quibbled on the technical merits of whether the act was a direct or indirect tax, he largely presented a colonial view that mirrored his opinion from the Albany Congress.

Parliament repealed the act and Grenville had to resign. The colonists had won. England didn't know it at the time, but the revolution was over. As any parent can tell you, once Parliament had given in to their whining, screaming baby pitching a fit to get his or her way, the colonists assumed that future decisions would be made through them. And, if the wrong decision would be made, then the colonists knew if they cried loud enough, the government would back down. Unfortunately for the British, they never understood that they had made the parenting mistake nor that for many colonists, the relationship between parent and child could never be the same again.

Seven

The American Revolution, pt. 2

As the dust of the Stamp Act situation settled, one important fact to note is that, in reality, the concerns were never really about representation. Or, to say it another way, the colonists were in the process of redefining ideas and concepts about life. More and more Americans were coming to realize this change. Not only were they redefining what representation meant in a free society, they were also redefining the concept of trade. No longer were they content to accept the ideas of mercantilism, the prevailing economic theory of Europe, but were embracing free trade, early capitalism. Of course, Adam Smith had not yet written *Wealth of Nations*—that happened also in 1776—but the Americans were advancing a view that suggested people should be able to trade with whomever they wished in order to get the best price they wanted.

Unfortunately for England, no one in the government could really comprehend what was happening. In fact, King George would struggle with 3 different Prime Ministers in the next 4 years and none of them would come close to understanding what was happening. In an attempt to still solve the debt problem, and to call Franklin's ideas about economics into question, the next Chancellor of the Exchequer would pass tariffs on a multitude of items. This, not surprisingly, did not make anyone happy, though for the next 2 years the issue would only rumble under the surface.

Partially, the complaints stayed somewhat muted because there still was a majority of citizens who were perfectly happy as British citizens. To protect those citizens from the terrorist groups trying to inflame the situation, the government pulled many of the frontier troops back into the towns. While the logic of this is easy to see, to the patriot rebels, this was more evidence that the Crown was determined to limit their freedoms. Thus, in 1770, Sam Adams was able to manufacture yet another crisis, the infamous Boston Massacre.

By early 1770, Adams had, along with John Hancock and Paul Revere, helped build tensions between the soldiers to an all-time high. In March, an incident between a mob and a single sentry turned violent as the crowd grew, so a small squad of reinforcements came to the aid of their fellow soldier. Eventually, in the shouting chaos of curses and rocks being thrown, a shot rang out and five Bostonians were killed. While the event certainly was a tragedy, as I tell my students, only one of those two words in the title is accurate . . . and the issue did happen in Boston. This was no deliberate massacre.

Yet, Paul Revere would quickly capitalize by producing a propaganda piece that told the colonists' side of the story and, before anyone in London ever heard of the event, all 13 colonies were in uproar over "the massacre." From Revere's account, the British had a full complement of soldiers, including snipers in windows, to attack a mostly peaceful demonstration. Back in London, when news came, yet another government fell and again, Parliament would repeal the various Townshend Acts. The complaining of the "children" in the 13 colonies had worked again.

At this point, King George turned to Lord North to be the next Prime Minister. North was clearly aware of how things seemed to be spiraling out of control and thus worked to calm things down. He approved the repeal of the various Townshend Acts. In an act of some political skill, he agreed with the decision to maintain one of the taxes, though—the tax on tea. Few in America complained, and over the next three years of silence, all appeared to have been solved. It wasn't; both Sam Adams and George III, both believed that they had been denied their ultimate victory. Still, unless something major happened, things might have ended here.

Then, just as with the sudden death of King Charles II in 1685, a surprising event sent events spiraling out of control. In 1773, Lord North decided to introduce a new Tea Act. His reasoning had nothing to do with the colonies, but rather the young East India Tea Company that was working to consolidate control on the subcontinent that England had taken at the end of the Seven Years War. Now, some ten years later, the Company was in dire shape economically and British control could be in peril, so North decided to act.

In an effort to help the Company cut their costs, he was going to allow them to ship tea directly to locations like the colonies and in the process, cut down the tariff costs. Previously, by landing first in England, the Company had to raise their prices to cover the tariffs. In North's mind, this would take care of many issues. First, it would lower prices for the Company, and thus be cheaper for consumers. Second, with the lower price, the tea should appeal even more to American colonists, thus securing their acquiescence to the idea of the British Parliament's control in government. Third, the lower price would undercut smugglers in America, which were also hurting the British idea of mercantilism. North had no idea how far he misread the effect of these actions.

In the fall of 1773, ships made their way for the main harbors in America, including Charles Town (modern Charleston), Philadelphia, New York and Boston. Up and down the seaboard, Adams had raised the Sons of Liberty and other protest groups again, bringing quick threats to the port cities. In every location, royal governors quickly decided to turn the ships away rather than risk open rebellion. Every location, that is, but Boston. There, royal Governor Thomas Hutchinson was determined to make Lord North's point.

As you probably remember from school, what happened next became one of the most famous moments in US history. Dozens of men, dressed as Mohawk Indians, boarded the British ships and threw the tea overboard. From this moment on, the conflict with the King was inevitable.

Parliament reacted with a measured, though predictable, series of acts to punish Boston. However, the colonists understood the Coercive Acts as aimed at all of them and determined to reject what they called the Intolerable Acts. Representatives from the colonies met in Philadelphia in the First Continental Congress in 1774. Meanwhile British General Thomas Gage was determined to keep the peace in Boston, so he began to track down where the rebels had stored up weapons and ammunition. One of these locations was determined to be in Concord, 20 miles outside of

Boston, so in the spring of 1775, he sent troops to find the weapons.

The resulting conflict was in reality the first battle of what would be known later as the War for American Independence or the America Revolution. Gage's troops would find no weapons, since spies (including Gage's own American wife) had reported the troop movement. Hundreds of militiamen would descend on Boston, effectively trapping Gage in the city. Meanwhile, down in Philadelphia, a second gathering of colonial representatives met in the Second Continental Congress. This group would vote in June of 1775 to create an army under the command of the same Virginian whose actions had kicked off this "road to revolution" some 21 years earlier. In January of 1776, a little known writer named Thomas Paine published a blockbuster called *Common Sense* that critically shaped public opinion. Then, in the summer of '76, while George Washington prepared to fend off a British invasion in New York, the Congress would pass their legal explanation of their actions, the Declaration of Independence.

Just as in London 90 years before, revolutionary leaders had reached their breaking point and actions had been taken from which there was no turning back. Unlike the 1680s though, not everyone was in agreement with the actions of rebels like Sam Adams and many Loyalists would fight in this "civil war" against their patriot neighbors. The next five years would be brutal in fighting; England would ultimately determine that they were bogged down in an unwinnable war and would accept the inevitable. At the same time, political leaders were soon coming to find out that though they agreed with getting rid of the King, they did not agree with what exactly they wanted to do to govern the new country. In fact, they weren't exactly in agreement to what kind of "new world" they wanted to create. Were they creating a new single nation, or merely getting rid of one overlord in order to have thirteen separate nations merely confederated together?

Eight

The US Civil War

One of the big myths that modern Americans hold is that "once upon a time," all Americans were happily united. Then, the evil of slavery showed up to poison our happiness and a few ugly, racist Southerners used this moment to try and destroy the country. The truth is far more complicated than that, and if any of the previous Great Crisis moments are like our own day, this is the one. In simple terms, there emerged in the country a philosophical divide that simply could not be bridged by political means.

In the first chapter, I told the story of how John Brown had come to determine that he must act, hoping to push the country to end the scourge of slavery. There is some evidence that Brown was hoping to be captured, or at least he assumed he might get captured. His raid and subsequent execution in December 1859 electrified the country and electoral process of that year. The Republicans, the former 4th party (5th party if you count the other anti-slavery groups) of the 1856 election, took Brown's actions as part of a rallying cry. The events leading to Brown's raid and subsequent execution were ones that unfolded, cause and effect, in similar fashion to the previous two crises.

Using skillful campaign tactics, the main Republican candidates presented themselves as the best solution to end the Democratic control under President Buchanan who had done little to end the growing antagonism between the north and the south. Those Republican leaders all were strong abolitionists, but they were able to rally much of the northern citizens to their party on the charge that the Southerners were out of control. The decision to execute Brown on a state law of Virginia seemed to many in the north as evidence that Southerners were no longer eager to work for compromise for the betterment of the country. To northern leaders, they felt as if Southerners had abandoned the Republic.

To Southern leaders, they saw the John Brown event in starkly different tones. From their perspective, it was northerners who had moved resolutely away from the concept of a free government, small and controlled by the people through their state governments. This description was, to them, the core of Thomas Jefferson's vision of a republic. That idea of the republic had been born and defined through a certain understanding of events from the previous seven decades. And, believe it or not, the Southerners had a legitimate point to be made, based on what had transpired.

From the start of the country, it is clear that there was no unified agreement as to what the Revolution had wrought. Though most "Patriots" had ultimately been happy to remove control of the mother country, England, there was no clear direction for "what's next." They knew that they wanted to prohibit anyone else from trying to control things, but, as they found out in the first decade of independence in the 1780s, if no one was really in control, then the group of states was close to being out of control. Meanwhile, the bigger nations of France, Spain and England were loosely circling in the hopes of making gains at the expense of the baby country.

Eventually a group of leaders performed their own version of a revolution, the creation of the Constitution. But this act was opposed by revolutionary heroes we know well—Sam Adams, Patrick Henry, Thomas Paine, John Hancock among them. Yet, after the success of the start of the new Constitution, largely dependent on having that now older famous Virginian, George Washington, as the figurehead, the supporters of the new government still argued over its power and scope.

For the next 60 years, from 1790 to 1850, the country would move ahead, often through key compromises, but with the question of control never fully resolved. Jefferson had taken over in his own "Revolution of 1800," but then as he governed, his own actions affirmed some of the need for increased power in the central government. The Supreme Court's decisions, and new dynamic powerful leaders like Andrew Jackson and Henry Clay, only solidified more centralized power and control. Yet even Clay and Jackson had not fully agreed, spending 20 years fighting about the levels of power in Washington DC, accusing one another of being evil, ruining the Republic. By 1850, in Clay's last years of life, the spirit of compromise was fully dying due to twin pressures: manifest destiny and abolition.

In the 1820s, a Second Great Awakening spread across the country, about 80 years after the First Great Awakening had played a key role in the last cycle of history. A major outcome of the spiritual movement was to bring to the surface a new series of social leaders who refused to be silenced about slavery. In 1820, a challenge to the national leadership emerged as citizens living west of the Mississippi river prepared to become a new state, the state of Missouri. Those citizens wished to affirm their openness to slavery. The crisis that emerged was skillfully navigated by leaders like Clay. As the Second Great Awakening flourished, the new abolition leaders were determined that the political leaders could not cover up slavery again.

While men like William Lloyd Garrison, William Still, Frederick Douglass, and James Birney were starting to publish and speak openly against abolition, a different outcome from the Great Awakening grabbed headline attention. The Great Awakenings have, in their roots, been a call to return to the "City on a Hill" belief of the special uniqueness of the United States, and connected to that, the need for brave new "pioneers" to take belief to untamed lands. The first Pilgrims and Puritans had crossed the oceans with this spirit. The responders of the First Great Awakening had crossed the Appalachian Mountains to spread our ideals through the middle part of the country. It was that notion that made Prime Minister Grenville's 1763 Proclamation Line such a fiasco. Now, in the early 1840s, it was a new generation's turn to cross the remainder of the continent. This new spirit took on the name of "Manifest Destiny."

Directly in the way of moving west, was the new country of Mexico, which had first achieved national independence in 1821, one year after the explosive Missouri Compromise. Over the next 20 years, she would struggle against major obstacles that the Anglos of the north had never really faced, such as the vast distances of the nation upon its birth. Hispanic settlements had been successful, but in disparate areas such as Sacramento, San Diego, Santé Fe, and

Mexico City, thus communication and coordination was very difficult. Eventually, the distance began to lead to political upheaval that resulted in various revolutions in Mexico.

Political control was seized by Antonio López de Santa Anna to try and bring stability to Mexico, but by the mid-1830s, restless citizens in Sacramento, Santé Fe and the most northern Mexican state close to the USA, Tejas, had all began to search for solutions in some form of independence. Santa Anna's position vis-à-vis Tejas was complicated by the presence of over 35,000 Americans who had taken on Mexican citizenship in exchange for bringing their plantation know-how to Mexico.

The resultant conflict between Mexico and Tejas, more recognizable by its anglicized name of Texas, would lead to an open war of independence by the Texans, both Anglo and Hispanic working together against Santa Anna. The success of this war came in 1836 with Santa Anna signing the Treaty of Velasco to end the conflict. Unfortunately, his signature was discredited in Mexico City where yet another revolution had led to the overthrow of Santa Anna's supporters. The new government quickly rejected the treaty and demanded Texas stay loyal to the nation. Texas, for its part, quickly appealed to the USA to be annexed, something that should have been an easy task for a Congress drunk on the manifest destiny wine.

However, the abolitionists finally saw their chance and worked tirelessly to oppose the acquisition of new land that clearly would be slave land. A new political party emerged, the Liberty Party, and it was successful in gaining some support for Congressional members and the choice of annexation was held in limbo. For Southerners, and many other citizens eager for more land, the position of the abolitionists was horrible, but year after year, annexing Texas was denied. This, to Southerners, was just more proof that the national government was moving away from the Jeffersonian view of a limited government. That abolitionists were involved only made the Southerners feel more worried; could it be possible that the national government might claim the same tyrannical powers that England had expressed 70 years before?

The election of 1844 became a critical moment in our story and perhaps the starting point of the clear unraveling period. The previous President, John Tyler had been pro-annexation but had been unsuccessful in his efforts. With the election of 1844 coming, it was clear that Tyler would not be brought back into the White House. The Democrats were planning to nominate the previous President, Martin van Buren, but as a New Yorker, there were questions of where he stood on Texas. The other party, the Whigs, was clearly going to support their great leader Henry Clay for a third run at the Presidency. To the Whigs, the issue was the economic stability of the nation and the government being more true to the founders' vision of the great men leading the country regardless of what the passions of the people wanted. Slavery was not chief among their concerns; most Whigs wanted Texas, but they wanted to be cautious and respectful to Mexico.

However, the issue of national power connected to slavery was not going to subside. During months of the summer of 1844, both Van Buren and Clay had been unclear on their position about slavery and annexation. For Van Buren, his answers meant that the Southern Democrats would not support him and during the Convention, the Democrats nominated Tennessean James Polk whose most redeeming feature was his rabid position on manifest destiny.

For Clay, his refusal to be totally clear would open the door for James Birney's Liberty Party to strike its strongest blow to date. As Clay attempted to hold onto the Whig strongholds and hopefully take New York, the abolitionists pushed the party to be more strident in opposing slavery. While most citizens were not at all interested in their liberal rhetoric, and most abolition leaders like Birney and Garrison had faced open northern opposition, some in the north began to sense that slavery was merely a convenient disguise for Southern leaders hoping to maintain control of the country. Clay would not come out strongly one way or the other for slavery, and continued to say openly that the Texas question needed to be handled in an honorable way. Many fans of Manifest Destiny heard Clay's words as code for not moving quickly for Texas.

Shockingly then to some pundits, Polk took the Presidency easily, though had Clay been stronger in New York in support of abolition, it is possible he would have taken the votes of the New

Yorkers. If he wins New York, he wins the Presidency and we possibly have no war with Mexico, nor the opening steps into the crisis. However, within weeks after the election, President Tyler signed annexation papers with incumbent Polk's approval. Northern Democrats, who had wanted to move cautiously and not just bulldoze the Mexicans, saw this move as a betrayal by the Southerner Polk. As soon as he took over in the White House in early 1845, Polk began to move ominously towards Mexico. For their part, the Mexican government had finally come to grips that they would never get Texas back, but they were determined to only lose the land north of the Nueces River.

A year later, Polk would provoke the Mexican nation into an unwise attack on American forces that had moved into the disputed land between the Nueces and the Rio Grande. Mexico, for her part, could look to the history of New Spain and find proof that Tejas had only been north of the Nueces. Texans, however, could also find support during the history of New Spain for the land extending to the Rio Grande. Not surprisingly, Polk and other manifest destiny adherents wanted every inch of the land formerly held by Spain.

Polk carefully positioned his troops, including the US Navy off the California coast and Army troops north of Santé Fe and also in the Oregon Territory. Once the shooting started, the war would prove to be something of a "pre-season" game for the men of the eventual Civil War. Mexico really never stood a chance, and the independence minded residents of all of northern Mexico never really opposed any American force, seemingly happy to join the United States. For our part though uncovering the pattern of the Great Crises, the Mexican War plays the same role as the French and Indian war in the previous story (or the Restoration from the first pattern we reviewed)—a glorious moment that seemed to portend good ahead, but really was only setting the table for the events that would unfold over the next decade.

Nine

The US Civil War, pt. 2

In 1848, the Mexican-American war came to its messy end with the signing of the Treaty of Guadalupe-Hidalgo. Many Americans then and now felt that Polk had bullied Mexico into the war and most were happy to have the experience over. Much like 80 years before with the end of the French and Indian War, most people assumed the country would move forward with success. Had they been looking more deeply, they would have seen the same sorts of events coming that the British leaders had missed.

The war had provoked a very strong anti-war reaction, mostly by the abolition leaders who were loudly protesting that the war was fought only to advance slavery. Southerners were not necessarily denying the point, though they would have hid behind the rhetoric of Manifest Destiny. The success of the war had netted the USA all of the land north of the Rio Grande River as well as the land directly west from that river, all the way to the Pacific Ocean. Leaders now wondered what to do next?

Just as Prime Minister Grenville discovered, trying to enforce rules about who could move where was problematic. Moreover, as Southerners listened to the words of the abolitionists, whose writings were often printed more widely in the South than elsewhere as evidence of their strident views, many in the South began to worry that their view of the government was being threatened.

To their perspective, everything the old Patriots had fought for was summed up in the idea of not being under the control of some monolithic government. The idea that this government could decide what could or could not take place in some local region of the country smacked Southern leaders as precisely what the British had been doing with their various taxing "acts" of the 1760s. The unwillingness of Congress to quickly annex Texas was all the proof they needed; Southerners believed it was obvious that taking that land would benefit the country. Thus, a group of abolitionist leaders within the government who were able to stop a natural positive act were clearly a threat.

The Compromise of 1850 proved to be as explosive as the Stamp Act. The idea was to cover the various problems inherent with the new land in one large act, much like they had dealt with the Missouri issue 30 years before. It was not to be. That defeat would be the last political gasp of the great political leaders of the previous half-century; men like Henry Clay and Daniel Webster. So, just as the British had struggled to find good political leadership, so too the Americans entered this new decade with a younger crop of leaders. Worse, most of them came to DC unwilling to embrace the old concept of compromise. These new leaders weren't all bad, of course, and one, Steven Douglas would take charge of moving a new version of the Compromise through Congress, albeit in pieces.

When he was finished, no one was really happy, and the enduring legacy would be the new Fugitive Act of 1850. The harshness of the act would be felt throughout the decade, and as we saw in the first chapter, would finally explode in Oberlin. Perhaps the act would not have been as impacting were it not for the political writing of Harriett Beecher Stowe. Much like Paine's 1776 writing, her words in *Uncle Tom's Cabin* struck a nerve across the land. The books sold 500,000 copies by 1853 and proved to be main reason that public opinion in the north turned.

However, just like before, it was a somewhat unrelated event that really got events moving. When Lord North signed off on that new Tea Act, he was not very concerned about the ramifications in the colonies. Senator Douglass was going to have the same experience in 1853. In 1849, the year after the victory of Mexico, gold was discovered in northern California, so that by 1855, over 300,000 people had moved to seek their fortune. California quickly became a state in 1850 as part of the compromise, but its explosive growth (in the 1840s, only approximately 60-70,000 people were in the state; 90,000 alone moved to California in 1850). It didn't take long before the conversation began about connecting the East and the West through a transcontinental railroad.

The Railroad would become the dominant industrial technological development in the US during the 19th century, but its beginning in the US was inauspicious. After losing a famous race with a horse, the railroad of the 1830s had not impressed many, but by the 1840s, the obvious advantages had taken hold. By 1850, more railroad line had been laid in the eastern US than in all of Europe. By 1853 Congress was ready to unleash the Army Corps of Engineers under the leadership of Secretary of War Jefferson Davis from Mississippi. The eventual report demonstrated that there were four key routes and each would eventually hold an east-west RR line, but in the middle of the continent, around the 42nd parallel, lay another choice.

It was the land on this possible middle route that attracted the attention of many including political leaders in Illinois such as Abraham Lincoln and Stephen Douglas. These leaders and others could see the obvious, that if a transcontinental railroad was built in the middle of the country's land, that the terminus would most likely go through Illinois and a small city on Lake Michigan—Chicago. Douglas in particular could see that if he could get the middle railroad line developed, then he could position Illinois businesses to profit from the railroad. To make this happen, he would need to prod Congress to develop the territory land west of Missouri and the newer state of Iowa. So, in late 1853, Senator Augustus Dodge from Iowa introduced the bill to organize the remaining land from the old Louisiana Purchase into one territory, opening the way for the northern, middle route across the continent. Over the holiday, however, Douglas came realized that Southern leaders would never support this idea, so in January 1854, he tweaked the initial proposal to create two territories---Nebraska which lay near Iowa and Kansas which would lay directly west from Missouri, the most northern slave state. Moreover, he would take the idea of "popular sovereignty" from the Compromise of 1850 and apply it here. To Douglas' mind, it really didn't matter. He didn't think slavery could ever establish itself in what many people thought was the "Great American Desert." Little did he realize that in the years to come, that area would be the "breadbasket of the world."

Douglas also demonstrated a flaw in his observation by missing the growing animosity surrounding slavery itself. Not only were the abolitionists stunned and angry about what they perceived to be a betrayal of the old Missouri Compromise, thus ready to act to preserve free soil, slaveholders from across the south were equally ready for action and eager to take Kansas as their own. The resultant action through the remainder of 1854 would come to be known as "Bleeding Kansas." Much like the Boston Massacre and the action at Lexington and Concord, Bleeding Kansas is critical in the journey towards war because it was the start of bloodshed and fighting. In many ways, the conflicts there are the first battles of the Civil War, just as Lexington and Concord, or Bunker Hill were for the previous crisis period. The tension spread east quickly due to the increased speed of communication, and just like the old British government could not control the spread of information post-Boston Massacre, the men in Congress could not either. Things even reached the floor of Congress where Preston Brooks would savagely attack Charles Sumner, an advocate of abolition, beating him senseless with a walking cane. Before long, members of Congress were coming to the Capitol armed or with guards.

The events in Kansas also drove the final iteration of the abolition political parties. As we have seen, first the Liberty Party organized. Then, after the victory against Mexico, that group morphed into the Free Soil Party. They were successful in raising the standard of abolition when they convinced Martin van Buren to run as their candidate in 1848. Politically, the bleeding Kansas events were a boon to the abolitionists as many northerners, mostly bystanders with no real opinion, were convinced that Southerners were now going to advance slavery no matter what, perhaps even trying to bring slavery into the north.

Many of the abolition leaders understood that they now had a great chance. The Whig party was in tatters, leaving a void in the US political spectrum. Another party, an anti-immigration party known more by its nickname, the "Know-Nothing Party" was taking shape in the northeast, but from New York to Illinois, the anger about Kansas was palpable. But, these leaders realized that they needed a better name than just a cute comment about slavery. Though abolition would be the central focus of the party, to win they'd have to reach people more moderate in their views. Quickly, they noted their chance by taking the name that the Democrats had dropped in the 1830s---the Republicans.

The Republicans were Thomas Jefferson's party, the old opposition party against the Federalists. By all rights, the

Republicans in theory should have been the party in the South, the party of small government, but through the Presidency of Andrew Jackson, they had lost the taste for the name. I also think it was just a matter of convenience; calling themselves the Democratic-Republicans was too unwieldy. For the abolitionists, they could take the name, draw loose references back to Jefferson and have a name that people would recognize instantly.

In the Presidential election of 1856, the Republicans (literally the 5th party behind the Democrats, the Whigs, the Know-Nothings and the Free Soil parties) shocked everyone by coming in second. Southerners were not amused and made clear their opinion. Senator Robert Tombs from Georgia stated openly that if the Republicans won in 1856, "that the Union would be dissolved, and ought to be dissolved." Other Southern leaders voiced their negative opinion about a Republican victory. The handwriting was on the wall; all that was needed know was the dynamite and a spark.

That explosive material would come rapidly in the next 3 years, starting first with the Dred Scott Supreme Court case. The decision by the court, led by Chief Justice R. B. Taney struck down the old Missouri Compromise decision and opened the door for slavery to move anywhere in the country. The Senate election of 1858, building off of the Dred Scott decision, brought the former Whig, Abraham Lincoln, a moderate on slavery, to the consciousness of the country. Lincoln's moderate position, eloquently spoken, generated support across the north, and while true Republicans, abolitionists to the core, were wary of the tall man from Illinois, they understood he might be the vehicle to the White House.

This was the period in 1858 that I wrote about in the first chapter. While Lincoln was debating Senator Douglas, the incident in Oberlin happened. Northerners rejoiced and "The Rescuers" went on speaking tours. Southerners became more worried and wondered what to do next. Then, the native son from Oberlin, recently back from activity in the Bleeding Kansas battles, John Brown, took his passion to Virginia. When Lincoln was elected President in November 1860, having never even appeared on the ballot in most Southern states, it didn't take leaders long in the Deep South to begin making plans. On December 17th, leaders met in Columbia SC to discuss their options. After moving the convention to Charleston, the leaders voted on Christmas Eve to secede. Two weeks later in early January, Georgia joined the movement and the march to open warfare would unfold through April 1861 when the first shots rang out against the Fort Sumter outside of Charleston.

Three more months brought early, smaller military actions, and then on July 21st, the First Battle of Bull Run became the first major engagement. Some 86 years before, on June 17, 1775, the fighting on Bunker Hill had ended. That battle had led into the conflict that would create the United States around a set of principles that were developed due to the events of the previous 90 years, the Glorious Revolution. Those principles were that no central government could dictate to the people, that rather power of government derives from the people. Yet the American Revolution also set forth another set of values relative to the experience of people, that of basic human liberty. In other words, not only did power derive from the people, it did so because at their heart, they are free beings created by God. The resultant eight decades did not, perhaps could not, solve the riddle of government mixed with slavery, the conundrum about the extent of the power of government.

Over the next four years, the north would win the civil war. Lincoln, however, to achieve victory, would further unleash the federal government. He would wage an undeclared war. He would suspend *habeas corpus*, twice. He would, as Andrew Jackson did, ignore the determinations of the Supreme Court and suggest that the Chief Justice should be arrested. In other words, to save the country, Lincoln would lead the greatest, perhaps worst, change to the government since Andrew Jackson's two terms in office. In the coming years, as the country emerged through the challenge of Reconstruction, the children born into the wreckage of the country, would come to expect that government to fix more and more things. The idea of the old American dream of individuals living free, "king of their own castle" would fall by the wayside in the wake of the explosive Industrial Revolution. That demand to see the government act more would ultimately lead to the next crisis, a dual-headed monster, a crisis within and without.

Ten

The Great Depression and World War II

Through the first two hundred and seventy-five years of English speaking existence in North America, 1608 – 1883, the general idea of coming to the New World was to come to find wide open spaces and a sense of freedom and independence unknown in Europe, even in England were the small size of the island prohibited easy access to land. Americans, as the citizens of the United States called themselves, could generally provide for all of their needs. However, in the next forty years, everything would change; by 1923 half of the country lived in urban areas, no longer "one with the land" or "living off the land."

This upheaval was caused by the Industrial Revolution. Historians debate exactly when and how the event fully happened, but suffice it to say that through the 19th century, concepts of industrialism were building, mostly in England. There, an impact was an explosion of urban centers built around industry. In the United States, the transcontinental railroad that we saw contributed to the coming Civil War became the dominant force in the country for the next 60 years, provoking a late 19th century explosion of more "industrial revolution." Post-war, as the country came to grips with Reconstruction and the continued march of Manifest Destiny to fully dominate the west, the large, national corporations grew in the 1870-1910 period.

Not surprisingly, these corporations operated in the same basic freedom that individuals had in starting their various businesses. Yet, the combination of national entities and industrial power led to economic growth hitherto unknown in the country. It was in that setting that individuals began to worry about their own independence as more and more goods, and the prices for those goods, were determined by factors and people existing far beyond their farm or house.

As urbanism exploded in the US, the cities were largely unprepared for this rush of people. You have to keep in mind the journey we have taken in this book. The desire for personal freedom that fueled the 275 years of development in North America meant that the government did not, could not, dictate to the people. Government, as an active visible construct was still largely an unknown factor except in places such as the Reconstruction South; after the Compromise of 1877, it disappeared in the South as well. Even in the 1880s, most people "saw" the government only at the Post Office. This was the ultimate creation of the Founders.

Yet, in a setting where thousands of people lived on top of one another, where there wasn't any simple water supply, where food could not be easily grown, questions about responsibility for things like health care, crime prevention, clean water, fire prevention or even education had no easy answer without government. Thus, while rural citizens were concerned about the growth of economic power of corporations and the seeming erosion of "life as we have known it," urban citizens were feeling a different kind of oppression relative to quality of life.

Under President Lincoln during the war, and in the South in Reconstruction under President Johnson and Grant, the national government had expanded its reach and influence. But over the next 20 years into the 1890s, that expansion of Federal power did not grow further. However, something else did grow—corruption in government. Up till the Civil War, choosing to be someone who served the country politically had been a noble undertaking. Few men (and it was always men at that time) ever served their entire lives; those that did, men like John Quincy Adams, Daniel Webster, Henry Clay or Stephen Douglas, were among the best and brightest. Certainly, pre-Civil War, there was occasional corruption and cronyism, perhaps worst with Andrew Jackson. Yet, largely, there is no record of overwhelming corruption that was the "rule of the day."

So, at a time when the average citizen felt as though everything was changing, and that their own sense of independence and freedom were at stake, the government seemed to have only leaders who were out for their own benefit. This failure of leadership only exacerbated the opinion among many that more change needed to occur. The push for change would emerge first from the plains of Middle America, but would soon be joined by workers from the urban north. Leaders and reformers like Jane Addams and Jacob Riis would begin trying to raise the consciousness needed for change in the urban cities. They and other groups of concerned citizens would coalesce in the 1880s around a new political party, the Populists.

From the late 1870s through 1896, the Populists, like the Abolitionists before them, would move slowly, creating momentum through consistency. By the 1896 election, there was some evidence that if they handled this election well, that they could supplant the Democrats as the number two party. The election of 1896 would be similar to that of 1856 when the Republicans erupted on the scene. However, it was not to be.

At the 1896 Democratic convention, a young politician, William Jennings Bryan, exploded onto the scene. Much like then Senator Barak Obama's electrifying moment in the 2004 Democratic convention, Bryan took the convention by storm. Unlike 2004, however, the rules were very different at that time regarding nominations and Bryan was surprisingly chosen as the Party's nominee (as many Democrats in 2004 wished could have happened with Obama). Bryan's power came not just from his brilliance as a speaker, but his topic. He addressed the Convention using the same language as the Populists; in effect, he stole their thunder.

The Populists had waited to hold their convention, assuming both the Democrats and the Republicans would nominate fairly normal candidates. Then, they believed, they could ride into the homes of average Americans with their explosive new ideas. See, the Populists were radicals of the time, and largely, their number one agenda was spreading Democracy. To them, the ills of the country, including the corruption with government, could be healed through more government, leadership that could be controlled through more Democracy. At the time, only male property owners could vote, though the 15th Amendment had altered that to open voting to all men, white or black. In the South, Democrats made sure that the newly freed slaves would not be allowed to vote and by the 1880s, the South was a single-party system. Still, the overall percentage of voters was very low compared to overall population in the country, so the Populists hopped on the "Democracy is best" bandwagon that was gaining steam worldwide.

Of course, while not the focus of this paper, as we have alluded to previously, Democracy was NOT what the Founders had intended. The men who wrote the Constitution believed that most people were ill equipped to accurately participate in governing. They believed that Democracy gives way to "mob rule" and a situation where minority opinions could never gain a fair hearing. In fact, the general evidence of participation in voting would seem to support the Founders. James Madison claimed that Democracy were explosive and would not protect private property. However, in the 1880s, the Populists thought that more democracy would protect average people.

The candidacy of Bryan, however, doomed the Populists as a party. . .but not their ideals. In the 1900 election, the Populists were nowhere to be seen, and the Democratic Party started its move from most conservative party to most progressive party. Yet, in the early 1900s, another term was being used to explain the new sense of activism that was sweeping the country—Progressivism. The Progressive movement would become the poster child for the changes emerging from the previous era of the Gilded Age. The majority of those ideas were concepts that started with the Populists, including women's suffrage, national income tax, direct election of US Senators and an 8-hour work day.

By the time we made our way through World War I, the country's mood had completely shifted away from the Founders' vision. Now, general feeling about the government was that of an activist, energetic government, largely created by Lincoln. Taxes became the norm in the country with the creation of the national income tax while many cities had their own tax of some sort, income or sales. Government regulation began, first against the Railroad in 1887, then throughout business. The Progressive movement would lead to a trio of Presidents—Theodore Roosevelt,

William Howard Taft and Woodrow Wilson—who championed more and more progressive ideas.

Wilson would ultimately lead the country through World War I that would dampen many citizens' support for Progressivism. Wilson's decision to get into the war was mostly an expression of the values of the Progressive Movement. All three Progressive Presidents had taken the country into more aggressive position in foreign policy decisions, both in our hemisphere and into the Pacific. Now, after the war, the country seemed to explode in a raucous period of living called The Roaring Twenties.

However, there were still serious issues relative to how citizens succeeded, found independence, or experienced their role in the country. They didn't know it when the 1928 election took place, but the cycle had once again taken place, moving the country through the High of the post-Civil War years, then the Third Great Awakening fed the progressive energy, and after that, the Unraveling of the World War I era. Though the hopes of the Populists had come true, life was not really much better. A huge disparity in income among the citizens was hidden behind the new creation of installment purchasing. The promises of more democracy had not really brought any real change in politics. Government was bigger, supposedly doing more to protect the citizen in broad general terms, but things were still very tough for the rural citizens as well as urban poor. Corruption still seemed ever-present, and though Democracy had promised to decrease the impact of money on elections, the reverse was more true---now money could more easily sway the masses to their bidding and the start of "Senators for life" was upon us.

Much like we have seen with the French and Indian War and the Mexican-American War, World War I seemed like a great success. But, as the unraveling continued, many people began to sense that something was wrong. A gamble had been made to tweak the system of the Founders through a series of governing decisions, including several Constitutional amendments. Though it wasn't clear at the time, cracks in the foundation of "normal" life would prove destructive in both domestic and international arenas.

Eleven

The Great Depression and World War II, pt. 2

Of all the American saeculums that we've looked at, this one and our current one are the most difficult to dissect. Partially they are more difficult because of the challenges inherent to the field of history. The closer we move to actual time, the harder it is for anyone to know anything about history. My own rule of thumb is that it takes at least 50 years to pass, but in reality, it could be a lot longer. Even now, experts from the Civil War period are still reconsidering concepts and ideas about the events and people of that era. In the last decade, there has been a burst of new scholarship about the Founders, people who lived over 230 years ago. I don't mean just new books, but entirely new positions about the meaning of their lives. So, when we start looking for the pattern of events leading into the crisis of the Great Depression and WW2, it's challenging to see everything clearly.

Moreover, the sheer breadth and amount of material that we have makes it increasingly complicated to provide a cursory overview—the very thing I have been doing in these chapters. We have so much information about World War II that one could start watching footage, just documentary footage, and not end for many more years, perhaps even longer than the actual 4 years of the USA part of the war.

One more challenge confronts us here—as the post-war era emerged, it was clear that technology was changing the speed of communication and action. What that meant for the USA was that no longer was she merely her own little country dealing with the issues of just her region. The same was true for the entire world. India, Japan, Serbia, South Africa, Egypt and so on—these countries also found themselves caught up in the fast paced world.

This, as we know, is still one of the growing issues of our own day in the early 21st century. There is simply so much information moving so quickly that no country can try to deal with "their own issues." For the USA, this last saeculum, our crisis was not going to only be something happening within our own borders. The crisis would emerge from afar, and the end result, once again, changed everything related to how the country both understood itself domestically and internationally.

The reality that speed of communication globally was going to be an issue was never more apparent than on Black Thursday in 1929. Things moved so quickly that people were able to hear about the implosion in their economic lives while travelling on ocean liners. Of course, the sheer amount of information also overwhelmed the system so that eight hours after the Stock Market closed, the ticker tape was still tapping out the bad news. Though there were some hopes of recovery over the weekend, Black Tuesday, October 29, dropped the bottom out. As the country reeled, President Hoover acted like the Presidents of old; he did little. Unfortunately for him, the country had changed so much that doing little was not going to work in the minds of the people.

Just like the period of the 1750s-1770s when the colonies had changed yet the Parliament could not comprehend those changes--thus their political decisions were consistently bound for conflict--the decisions from Congress over the next 2 years only made the Depression worse. By 1932, Hoover himself brought forth important changes, increasing national work programs as well as direct aid to the poor, yet those changes were too little too late. Over the summer, developments clearly indicated that Hoover would be unable to manage the situation, with the worst being how the veterans of World War I were treated during the Bonus Army fiasco.

The election in 1932 opened the door for Franklin Delano Roosevelt to become President. Unlike his cousin Theodore, he would run as a Democrat, but much like TR, he was a Progressive through and through. He understood, in ways Hoover never seemed to, that the people were expecting more from government. Hoover tried to appeal to the America of the 1870s, of the 1830s— to be self-reliant, to pull together as communities. FDR understood that the Americans of the 1930s had become dependent on government, and assumed Congress would do more. And, boy, did he do more.

Between 1933 and 1936, FDR unleashed what was known as the New Deal. In short, he did everything Hoover had tried-- cheerleading, aid to big businesses, federal work projects, aid to farmers, aid for mortgages, direct aid to the poor—he just did more. The difference between Hoover and FDR is not in their actions, but in a matter of degree. FDR tried anything and everything, starting and stopping programs, and he did them in huge amounts. The bad news, though, was that nothing FDR did really worked any better than Hoover.

Yes, by 1934, unemployment was lower (though in FDR's first year, unemployment reached 25%), and more people had some sort of financial aid, either in direct loans or some sort of government work project. So, if the question is "did FDR's actions make it better for various citizens in the short term," then yes, the New Deal worked. But, when asking if the new programs actually solved the problem, the evidence is clear that they did not. By the late 1930s, the economy was still stuck. Any attempt to stop government aid sent unemployment up and the economy down in a tailspin.

If we stopped the story here, we would have to conclude that for the first time, the crisis that we faced overwhelmed the country. The "war" was not fought to victory. Yet, as I had stated already, another strand must be woven to see the full overview of the journey to this crisis. Interestingly enough, the dates become very connected. FDR was elected to office in November of 1932, but the inauguration happened March 4, 1933. A month before, January 30, 1933, Adolf Hitler took office as the Chancellor of the German government, a position similar to the British Prime Minister—an elected official asked to create a government based on the popularity of the party within the national governing body, the Parliament in England, the Reichstag in Germany.

The success of the Nazi party in Germany, of course, is not the "start" of WW2. In fact, historians have argued for decades as to when one can trace the start of WW2. That question is, for Americans, even harder when one realizes that what we call World

War II was really two separate wars that merely happened coincidentally at the same time. In both cases, our war with Japan and the European war with Germany trace their full beginnings much earlier, even as far back as the late 1800s. For our purposes, it is easy enough to see how the conclusion of World War I set the major pieces in place.

The Treaty of Versailles is one of the most impacting diplomatic decisions in world history. Today, in 2011 as I write this now, we are still dealing with the results of that diplomatic fiasco. Japan, Russia, Italy, Korea, Vietnam, the Middle East, the Balkans and of course Germany all left 1919 angry at how they were treated, or ignored, by the dominant players in Paris: England, France and the USA. Worse, the USA Senate failed to ratify the very treaty that then President Woodrow Wilson had built. England left the conference economically weakened and militarily no longer able to police the world. France had been a shell of herself since the French Revolution and was now incapable of leading, having only succeeded in her arrogance to give Germany a reason for revenge.

In 1921, the Americans had demanded a naval arms reduction treaty, which only led to further conflict, as almost every other arms limitation treaty has done. It served to anger the Japanese and further weaken England, yet the US did not see any reason to take a more prominent position on the world stage. In the same year, Benito Mussolini was elected into Italy's national governing body, the Chamber of Deputies. The next year, 1922, he was asked to become the Prime Minister, making Italy the first fascist nation.

The 1920s were not "roaring" in Europe, and though the US attempted to help through a series of convoluted acts in the middle of the decade, the Depression sunk Europe to new lows. The German middle class, in particular, lost everything. Workers throughout Europe were turning to communism, the new and exciting version of socialism that had succeeded in taking over Russia in 1917. Others, both poor and the former middle class, were turning to the conservative socialism called "fascism," with its extremely loud calls of nationalism.

While Hoover struggled with the Depression in 1931, the Japanese marched into Manchuria, taking the province from a weak and divided China. Americans could have cared less, though the League of Nations, a precursor to the United Nations (and just as weak and ineffective, perhaps more so), did attempt to halt Japan and Italy (who was equally looking at North Africa for its own room to grow). By 1933, both Japan and Germany left the League.

By the time 1935 rolled around and FDR was planning for his second run for office, Italy had invaded Ethiopia, an decision that built a stronger relationship between Italy and Germany, now both "outsiders." Congress would pass its first Neutrality Act in 1935, then another in the election year of 1936. Germany started to show her cards by moving troops into the Rhineland, that stretch of land on the West of the Rhine neighboring France.

For Hitler, this was merely the start of his efforts to rebuild Germany. Certainly, he had clear, horrific plans in mind for racial cleansing in Germany, and he did want to grow the country, the idea he called *Lebensraum*. Yet, in many respects, he was facing the same problem as FDR—how to restart a broken economy. Just like FDR, he turned to work projects, so the *autobahn* was born. Like FDR, he supported larger industries, so *Volkswagon* started rolling small little beetle-looking cars off the assembly line. Unlike FDR, Hitler plans worked well; the country's economy roared, thus Hitler knew that to maintain control, he had to keep the people happy. He seemed to understand well, perhaps better than FDR, that war always helped an economy.

FDR would start to see this first hand when the US economy rolled back into another Recession in 1937. By 1938, FDR understood how important military spending could be for the country and he began seeking ways to moderate the initially tougher Neutrality Acts. What started as a total ban with warring nations became a kind of "cash and carry" act. By 1939-1940, we were actively lending military aid to the "good guys." Not surprisingly, the US economy would pick up steam. It did so at a fortuitous time.

Between 1937-1939, the world raced towards more open conflict. Hitler had his troops involved in the Spanish Civil War, giving his generals a sort of "pre-season" game while England and France stayed home. He would unite with Austria, take back German land from the darling of the Versailles crowd,

Czechoslovakia, then use the appeasement of the British Prime Minister as an allowance to take the rest of the Czech land (setting Slovakia free, as she had wished to be back in 1919). In the spring of 1939, Germany would invade Prague, then on the first of September, after being rebuffed by a surprisingly resilient Poland, he would invaded that country.

Russia, another "outcast" from the Versailles debacle, would join Germany in ripping apart Poland. The Poles, for their part, had perhaps been set-up by British and French promises. Over the next two years, Germany and her friends in Europe (Russia and Italy) would dominate. The USA watched fearfully, all the while growing stronger economically by selling military supplies to the allies. She was also watching nervously to the Pacific where Japanese military leaders would overthrow their government in 1940.

1941 would become the year in which the rest of the world joined the war, as you probably already know. Germany, unable to destroy England, due to both English resilience, the protection of the English Channel and the military aid from the USA, turned on Russia. For Hitler, this was both a racial decision driven from his views shown in *Mein Kampf* as well as an economic decision. If war ceased, the German economy might start to slow. During the build up to war, and the first two war years, Germany was the strongest economy on earth. Not surprisingly, the German people were very happy with the leadership of Hitler, though perhaps a tad bit concerned about some of the social policies and rules. As long as Hitler could keep the good times rolling at home, the people would support him and perhaps ignore the many ominous signs. To keep those good times rolling, Hitler knew he had to keep the economy humming, and to do that, he needed war to happen. Plus, the Russians had plenty of raw materials, and if anything, World War 2 is largely about oil and industrial raw materials.

That need for supplies of industry was precisely why the Japanese finally, and perhaps fatally, decided to attack Pearl Harbor. Their movement into Manchuria had led, in the late 1930s, into full-scale war in China, and though there was not much resistance from the Chinese, there also was no organized government to actually surrender. Japan was not able to ever fully conquer every square mile of a country several times its size, and that country had no real leader able or willing to just surrender in the face of such terrible loss. To further prosecute the war, the Japanese needed more and more raw materials—oil, tin, rubber, metal, gasoline. For that, the Japanese needed the USA.

Or, they needed their own supply. They could get most of what they wanted in two places, north of them in lands controlled by Russia, or south of them in lands loosely controlled by England and the Netherlands. As the Japanese surveyed the landscape, though attacking Russia would help their ally Germany, attacking the islands to their south would be much easier. The only hitch in that direction was that the USA controlled the Philippines Islands, and the Japanese believed (probably erroneously) that the USA would attack them if they initiated any attack on the South Pacific islands.

Thus, on December 7 1941, while the Germans and the Russians grappled outside of Moscow, Japanese forces attacked the US Navy at Pearl Harbor in Hawaii. Though the initial shock was great, within 5 months, the tide had already been turned at the battle of Coral Sea in the spring of 1942, the Marine fights at Guadalcanal and the battle of Midway later in June 1942. Economically, the USA would explode with growth as millions of dollars, much of it newly minted or borrowed, were poured into industry. By 1945, 80 years after 1865, the war against the Great Depression and against the Axis would be over; the USA would emerge as one of the world's superpowers.

Yet, the cost was very high, both in human life and in the old American concepts of herself. Small federal government? Gone. Protection by our two great oceans? Gone. Simple capitalism? Gone. Aversion to standing armies? Gone. Limit to the destruction of man? Gone. George Washington's dream of no entangling alliances? Gone. FDR had indeed "saved" the country, both from economic disaster and dictatorial tyranny, but to do so, he had changed the country, and perhaps the entire world.

Twelve

Uncovering the Pattern

Earlier, I explained that the saeculum is a cycle that occurs over the period of (roughly) a human life—between 70-90 years. Remember, the entire point of the book is not merely to give you a history lesson, but to see if there is a pattern that can be discerned as we live through our own Fourth Turning, our own Great Crisis period. That we are in a crisis seems, to me, indisputable, but where are we? Was President Obama 2008 election the same as President Lincoln's 1860 election, or perhaps President Hoover's 1938 election? Is the economic meltdown that started in 2006 the actual crisis, just like the Great Depression was, or is it part of the road to crisis like the economic struggles experienced in the 1750-60s period? Will any of the current political writings, perhaps a book by Glenn Beck or by Al Gore, have the same impact as *Uncle Tom's Cabin?* Are we in the crisis (is it 1778, 1863, 1943) or are we approaching the crisis (is it 1770, 1857, 1930)?

It is likely that we will never know for sure till it is all over, or at least till the actual crisis is upon us. A truism from history is that the participants cannot see what the survivors know, especially what the surveyors report 25, 50, and 100 years later. When the summer of 1776 was over and the wounded from the battles in New York were in the process of being nursed to health, and the ink from the Declaration of Independence was barely drying on copies, most people experienced that September has they had through the previous years. They went to work, they harvested the fields, they prepared food for the winter, they went to church, they enjoyed relaxing activities with friends . . .in other words, little changed.

Sure, where the actual war happened, it was different. Yet, even there, people went about life in normal ways. As July 1, 1863 happened in Gettysburg, people still went to work, at least at first. People picked their vegetables in the garden, in some cases to ensure that they kept the goods rather than the army getting it. Back in the winter of 1777-78, then General Washington complained in his diary that the farmers and civilians living around Valley Forge acted as if there was no war. His army was malnourished, but the people living around him had plenty of food for the winter. So, as we go through these years, it is most likely that we will never really know when "it" happens.

Yet, the history that we have looked at can provide us some clues, especially through the pattern. We aren't looking for exactly the same sort of thing to happen at the same time. That would be unreasonable to assume. We've already seen that Thomas Paine's *Common Sense* came at the end of the road to the American Revolution, while Harriett Beecher Stowe's *Uncle Tom's Cabin* appeared at the start of the road to the Civil War. In the future, maybe we'll note that Michael Moore's *Fahrenheit 9/11* was the equivalent explosive writing when it came out in 2004. Or, maybe that honor will lie with Al Gore's *Inconvenient Truth* that appeared in 2006; perhaps, as with the road to the Great Depression/WW2, we won't see any one book (though *Mein Kampf* could hold that honor for that period).

The first most obvious concept from all 4 "road to crisis" journeys that we've seen is that **they all start with some sort of war:** the Dutch wars/King Philip's war, the French and Indian war, the Mexican-American war, and World War I. None of those wars were the great crisis; the clicking of the global tumblers had not fully hit, the generations were not in the correct alignment. Yet, each of those conflicts put forces in motion that led into the depths of the Great Crisis.

In the early journey into crisis, various attributes emerge related to government, governing and decisions. Though the country had moved successfully through war, those in charge were not able to handle the situation well. In other words, at the moment when the country needed the best, the wisest leaders, **the leadership in charge was at its weakest**. That is not to say that every Congressman, every President or member of Parliament were horrible, but in general terms the leadership exhibited poor decision making, especially when compared to those of 20 years before. More so, when compared to the leadership that emerged during the crisis itself, the leaders of the "road to crisis" seem very incapable, vacillating, and unsure.

The weakness of leadership becomes more apparent as we investigate the decisions that were made during the years of the "road to crisis." Certainly, at other points during each saeculum, bad political decisions were made, but the sheer number of **poor governing decisions** made overwhelm the system. It is almost as if the leaders simply cannot get out of their own way as they make one bad decision after another. This failure is exacerbated by a growing **sense of distance, or isolation, of the people from the government.** The current government attempts to put through various acts or laws, in some cases to deal with what it assumes to be normal "business as usual" and in other cases, to deal with an issue that emerged from the previous war. Regardless, the people's response to these decisions is almost universally opposition. In the 1670s, the Crown's attempt to push through a Declaration of Indulgence blindly missed how strongly people feared any movement towards Catholicism. Equally blind, Prime Minister Grenville's decisions to handle the debt of the country through a series of Acts to raise funds, culminating in the Stamp Act in 1765, were seen in the colonies as an attempt to steal their liberty. The 1850 laws comprising the Compromise of 1850 were loudly condemned from all sides, as were the laws of Congress passed under President Hoover as the Depression set in during 1929-1931, especially legislation relative to the experience of the farmers of America (they would experience the coming of the Depression years ahead of the actual event in 1929).

The choices of the government in question not only led to bumbling decisions, but **overt opposition**. At this point, the citizens in every crisis period were divided between verbal opposition and active opposition, but clearly the fact that they were going to oppose their own government must be noted. King Charles II had to avoid more than one assassination attempt and the members of Parliament were as fearful of the people. In 1685 the Monmouth Uprising became open opposition, just as the actions of groups like the Liberty Boys, the Green Mountain Boys and the Sons of Liberty did 80 years later in 1765. Ninety years later, the first of several rescues of captured freedmen, taken because of the Fugitive Slave Act from 1850, would take place in Boston. Seventy-seven years later, Milo Reno would lead his Farmer's Holiday Association to revolt against Hoover, while the more loosely organized Bonus Army followed men like Sergeant Walter Waters as they marched on Washington D.C. These groups were determined to fight for what they deemed their natural rights, something that needed to be protected.

From the vibrant over opposition to the poor governing decisions, **new political voices appear.** The various "Congresses" during the journey to the American Revolution gave rise to perhaps the greatest collection of political leaders in US history. Yet, they are at least matched with zeal by the new voices in Parliament in the late 1600s, particularly the new Whig party, during the road to the Glorious Revolution. The Republicans emerging in 1855 and the newly Progressive Democrats of the 1920s both shook up the established order of things politically and brought new ideas and concepts to the fore.

We have already mentioned the **key, explosive political writing,** but this point deserves a second look. John Locke's writings in the 1670s provided a sense of direction for those wanting a change; the idea that an absolute monarchy was not the best way forward had been discussed before, but Locke gave shape to the notion in ways that echoed in the hearts of the citizens. Obviously throughout the history of all of the "roads," there are several writings that are important. An entire book could be written about the impact of pamphlets and books in each journey, but as with Locke, the impact of Paine and Stowe cannot be overstated. And, while not American, Hitler's *Mein Kampf* was as powerful in Germany, propelling the country forward, and obviously impressing Americans (positively and negatively) since he was named *Time Magazine's* "Man of the Year" in 1938.

Another aspect visible from the patterns is that as we closed in on each Great Crisis, there had been a **significant change in communication.** Before the full crisis emerged, rapid communication had become the norm in a new and exciting way. Before the Glorious Revolution, pamphlet writing to express political views had become the norm. In the 1770s, the postal service of Benjamin Franklin had made communication between the 13 colonies a thing of beauty. When Paul Revere completed his propaganda masterpiece about the so-called Boston Massacre, the painting was seen up and down the East Coast weeks before London ever heard the news of the event. In 1851, the company Western Union started service and so, when the crisis of the Kansas-Nebraska hit, citizens in the slave-holding South or abolitionist area of New England knew about the shocking events within days. Quicker still, FDR was able to harness the radio, a technology that had exploded in popularity and use in the 1920s, during the darkest days of the Depression. Now, citizens could hear Edward R. Murrow speak to them live from the Battle of Britain or find solace in the soothing voice of Roosevelt in his fireside chats.

The Great Depression itself is another clue as **economic malaise or challenge** is one more common aspect to note. While the Depression itself can be considered to be the Crisis from the last saeculum, it can be noted that the Depression itself is merely a step ON THE ROAD to crisis when only looking at the international issues of the war. There is less economic crisis in the road to the Civil war, but clearly southerners felt that the threat to slavery was a potential economic disaster. And, there was an economic "panic" in 1857 that ruined many people's fortunes, including U. S. Grant. Grenville's bumbling early on the road to the American Revolution was due to the great debt that the country faced, just as it had been back in 1671-72. There, Parliament and Crown could only watch as England sank under great debt that led to the Financial Panic of 1672.

Another pattern point within the last three "roads" is **an explosive event that leads to a very controversial government response.** That response, in turn, proved to spark galvanizing action among the citizens. During the road to the American Revolution, the tea party (the explosive event) led to the British Parliament passing the Coercive Acts. These acts were very measured, limited, and from England's point of view, merely aimed at troublesome Boston. To the colonists, angry along the full Eastern seaboard, the "Intolerable Acts" were evidence of a government response aimed at every American. Immediately after this came arrival of Minutemen from various states and the gathering in Philadelphia. Similarly, after the raid on Harper's Ferry in 1858, the execution of John Brown, also considered measured by the Virginians, sparked action by both north and south. In the south, as we have already shown, the various state militias became the nucleus of the CSA army; in the north, Republicans were able to show the execution as evidence that the southerners were prepared to act against every American. Finally, in 1932, President Hoover and the Congress stumbled badly with the gathered veterans of the Bonus Army. Hoover's decision to send in the Washington DC police, and then the US Army was very controversial. Most Americans decided once and for all that Hoover, and the Republican Party, was out of touch with the needs of the citizens, which brought on the election of FDR (and Democrat Party dominance for 50 years).

The last two key concepts are the ones that perhaps should make us the most nervous: **"blood in the streets"** and **the "unforeseen trigger event."** When the US Army drove into the Bonus Army or when Hitler's forces rounded up 100s of Jews during *Kristallnacht,* that sense of open bloodshed should have been familiar to anyone paying attention to the pattern. Bleeding Kansas of 1854-55 was the same sort of event, even leading to bloodshed inside the Capitol Building the next year. The Boston Massacre in 1770 and the Monmouth Uprising both brought open bloodshed to the country.

Yet, each road to crisis seems to have a moment when all things could be saved and the crisis averted, were it not for a seemingly innocuous event. No one could had foreseen that when King Charles was tragically killed via a horse riding accident, his horse stepping into a gopher hole in 1685, that three short years later members of Parliament would invite an invading force under William of Orange to their shores. Prime Minister North's decision to help the East India Trading Company, and lower the price on tea in the colonies was simple enough, yet even most citizens living in the colonies had no idea that his decision in 1773 would lead, two years later to Lexington and Concord. In 1852-53, the choice of Congress to push for an transcontinental railroad was a "no-brainer" that would aid the country; clearly connecting the new lands of the far west back to the east made economic sense. Yet, that choice was the trigger for the fighting of the civil war to begin two years later in Kansas.

We are still perhaps too close to the last crisis road to discern where the unforeseen trigger lies—domestically or internationally. It could be the culmination of Progressive dreams with the amendment to the Constitution to prohibit alcohol. Prohibition opened a host of domestic changes, some for good and some for ill. It could be FDR's arrogant choice to attempt to pack the Supreme Court in 1936, which ultimately undermined his New Deal efforts. But the two more likely candidates came in the 1920s, one domestic and one international. Domestically, the 1920s saw the explosion of a new US consumer culture, with advertising hitherto unseen. That built a demand for goods that did not match actual wealth in the country, so began the march of consumer debt. This issue of personal debt contributed to the overall maldistribution of wealth that contributed to the depth of the Great Depression. Internationally, the US also made a kind and innocuous decision to help Germany economically with the Dawes Plan. The plan's main idea was that if Germany could be strengthened economically, then it would help all of Europe. Germany would be able to pay its Treaty of Versailles reparations payments back to England and France, who in turn, could pay off its debt to the US. That's right—ultimately we were paying ourselves back the money owed to us by giving economic help to Germany (in loans and encouraging US companies to invest in Germany). Not only did this help prepare the German economy and industrial foundation for what Hitler would do in the 1930s, worse, it tied the European economy to ours. Thus, when the Depression hit in 1929 here, it drug down all of Europe with it. As the economic nightmare unfolded, the feeling of complete financial loss and ruin allowed the German citizen to pursue radical alternatives to government (though Spain, France and England also toyed with similar extreme solutions).

These common happenings provide us with a template to consider our own times. As we march deeper in to the second decade of the 21st century, we must be watchful for these kinds of events. Some have not happened yet, others perhaps have. Are there matches with the previous "roads?" If so, what do you do about it?

To recap, look at the chart below. Each of these events comprises the steps on the road to crisis. They do not always occur in the same order, though all roads began with a victorious war for the nation. Obviously the actions of government had been different, relevant for the events of that time. Yet, within this chart, we can see a pattern that, if discerned to be occurring, would be a signal to prepare for our own Great Crisis.

The Common Attributes

1. War starting the conflict
2. Weak governmental leadership
3. Poor governing decisions
4. Feeling of distance between government and the people
5. Active opposition to government
6. New political voices
7. Explosive political writing
8. Significant change in communication
9. Economic distress
10. Explosive event→controversial government reaction→galvanized opposition
11. Blood in the streets
12. Unforeseen trigger event propelling government actions that lead to more tension

As we consider these attributes, a more ominous aspect must be considered. It's not like previous societies have not faced economic distress, a poor choice by the government or someone writing an impactful book that captured the attention of the country. Ultimately, as we study the history of the previous "roads to crisis," it becomes apparent that the biggest problem was that people lost the ability, or the desire, to compromise. The various sides simply lost the ability for discussion. The growing philosophical divide over whatever the issue was (religion, government style, representation, human rights, economic crisis) became so deep that no middle ground could be reached. As we move into the second decade of the 21st century, that reality of no room for compromise seems more and more obvious.

Thirteen

The Philosophical Divide

In May 1999, *Salon* ran an interview with then Governor George W. Bush. In the interview, Bush was asked about his success in his Texas election when other Republicans had done poorly. Bush answered in part, saying, "I showed the people of Texas that I'm a uniter, not a divider. I refuse to play the politics of putting people into groups and pitting one group against another." That use of the term "uniter, not a divider" was perhaps the first mention of the phrase that became quite popular through the increasingly strident first decade of the 2000s. Bush was constantly criticized for NOT actually uniting the country and rather pursuing policy choices, mostly in foreign policy, that divided the country.

If there is anything that I have learned in my years as a Professor of History is that we have only had a few times in our national story where the citizens were united. We weren't united in our choice to rebel against England. We weren't united in deciding on our early government. We weren't united in our wars against England in 1812, Mexico in 1848 or Spain in 1898. The harder you look, the more it becomes obvious that our system has actually provided more opportunity for division than for unity.

James Madison, the Father of the Constitution, actually saw this coming. As he contributed to the political writing supporting the new Constitution, what we call *The Federalist Papers,* he wrote the 10th article in November of 1787 commenting on this very question. Many opponents of the new proposed governing document argued that the new type of government, a Republic, had never been tried on a scale this large. They suggested that the size would doom the government. Some even thought that a Democracy might be better.

Madison disagreed strongly, as did almost all of the Founders. Not only did he argue that Democracy has "ever been spectacles of turbulence and contention; have ever been found incompatible with personal security or the rights of property;" but he saw a virtue in the Republic over a vast geographic size. In a country of that size, he proposed, the idea of division would strengthen the country. Madison saw that there would never be a time when everyone agreed with each other, at least not without some dictatorial power that would remove "the causes of faction. . .by destroying the liberty which is essential to its existence." But, in a government set up like our Republic, if you "take in a greater variety of parties and interests; you make it less probable that a majority of the whole will have a common motive to invade the rights of other citizens." In other words, certainly there will be division, but there will always be some equal counterweight that opposes that view. This principle of tensegrity (tension + integrity, often used in the world of architecture) would actually provide stability to the entire organization, much like a spider's web finds its structure by pulling apart from itself.

So, in short, we don't actually WANT a uniter. Someone who proposes to become a uniter, according to Madison's view, possibly could be deluded or worse, be someone who wishes to curtail our freedoms to achieve this aim of uniting. Still, the allure of unity is strong. Moreover, there have been times when we the country was more united than others—the twenty year period of the "High" that comes after the last Great Crisis.

Strauss and Howe saw this clearly in their writings; when everyone feels good for having made it through the last crisis, it is easy for unity to emerge. Looking only at American history, the time after Jefferson's election through the 1824 election is considered the one time when the nation didn't even have an effective second party. Jefferson's Republicans stood supreme in the "Era of Good Feelings." Post-Civil War, the sense of unification was shorter as the challenges of Reconstruction took hold, but even then, in the 1868-1880s period (especially in the West and North), there was a sense of everyone being on the same page. The war was over; slavery was dead; the idea of secession seemed dead as well—the business of the country became business. After World War II, the country again entered the High of the

Eisenhower years, happily on the same page, at least on the surface. While the nation had the challenge of the Cold War internationally, and the specter of nuclear war was very real, domestically, everyone seemed on the same page. The Presidents after FDR did little to try and turn back the clock, supporting more and more government programs and everyone was happy. Yet, this united sense again only lasted for about a decade and a half, till the early 1960s.

With each journey towards crisis, the ominous aspect that emerges is the fact that as the Fourth Turning comes closer, the two sides that emerge in contest over the country become philosophically divided. The story is the same whether we are looking at the 1760s or the 2010 period. Pundits and citizens search for unity, wish for a leader to unite the country, yet the various supporters of "the issue" grow so determined, so passionate about their view, that compromise is impossible. Older people will longingly remember the years of the previous High, when everyone "pulled together," but those years and that spirit is gone.

Henry Clay, one of our most important political leaders not to be a President, learned this lesson the hard way. His entire career, starting in the early 19th century, elected in the run-up to the War of 1812, had been built on compromise. He was known as "The Great Compromiser." Again and again, from his time in the US House of Representatives in 1806, he built consensus through compromise. So, when he saw the nation inching to implosion in the wake of the Mexican war in 1849, he assumed he could fix things. Slavery, to him, was merely a surmountable issue. He had achieved similar compromise over slavery before in 1820 with Missouri, why not now? Yet, when he introduced his plan in January 1850 it soon became clear that he was not living in 1820. In the intervening 30 years, the people on the two sides of the issue of slavery had grown too strident. For them, abolitionists on one side, state's right southerners defending their industry on the other side, there could be no compromise.

I believe we are not yet in our Great Crisis, though we are "on the road." I don't know that anyone, certainly not I, could articulate what the "issue" will be. Is it more Democracy? Is it a question of economic equity? The rights of others, whether the rights of the unborn or of the gay community? The environmental toll of so many humans on the planet? As a participant in the current history, it is nigh impossible to tell. Regardless there is a growing philosophical divide between Americans, loosely drawn between "conservative" and "liberal" citizens.

My point of writing, as I have said repeatedly, is to provide you enough warning to start thinking about your own views. As you do so, understand the times. Stop looking for a uniter to emerge politically. Not only is that concept faulty, based on Madison's own writings (and the evidence of the previous 230+ years), but also as we have now moved resolutely through our own saeculum, we be at that stage where uniting simply won't happen.

Madison said it better than I: "As long as the reason of man continues fallible, and he is at liberty to exercise it, different opinions will be formed." As the years take us further and further from the previous high, the willingness to listen diminishes and the willingness to fight grows. From the moment President Clinton ran into challenges of the moral kind, and the "Moral Majority" element of the conservative political right became strident, the rancor between the left and the right grew. Moveon.org came out in 1998 to support President Clinton and then led the charge against what they perceived as a stolen election in 2000. The Tea Party movement came out in 2009 against what they perceived as a President and Government who were determined to irreparably change the country.

This sense of "someone" "changing" the country, as I have said, is the core issue that compels us to stay aware. This is the reason any of this matters. After each Great Crisis, the country was changed. For better or worse depends, obviously, on your viewpoint, but change it did. You must be ready for this as it happens. I don't think you can stop it, but you can be prepared.

Fourteen

Looking for Matches

We've discovered that there are common attributes within the historical pattern of events leading to the Great Crisis that has come, regularly, every 80 years or so, for the past 400+ years. In no particular order, those common attributes are the random trigger event, a critical piece of political writing, blood in the streets, economic distress and it all begins with some war. Politically, weak governing leadership, new political voices, overt/active opposition to the government, and misguided governing decisions that indicate a growing distance between the government and the people impact the road to crisis, with a new explosive communication tool raising the pressure. And finally, one big explosive event leads to a controversial decision by the government that galvanizes citizens to the idea that active opposition was the only choice. Philosophically, all compromised had ceased. The divide was too great. So, the question we must now answer is "how many of the common attributes have we seen?"

That the journeys have all begun with war is somewhat ironic. In all four great crises, the country was successful in the wars. It's not as if we lost and then people were angry over the outcome, feeling a distaste for the loss of life and economic cost of war. No, the victory at each level was fairly complete, especially the French & Indian war and the Mexican-American war. But that fact that a national victory only exacerbating tensions is one piece of evidence that the war was not the crisis itself. Clearly this has been, or perhaps IS, our situation now. Regardless of how current Americans feel about the "War on Terror," President Bush's poorly phrased concept of our post-9/11 actions, we won. Militarily, the "war" with Iraq and the Taliban in the 2002-2004 years was a victory. And the victory was complete. Yet, just as in our previous pre-crisis wars, it is after the victory that tensions mounted. Afghanistan was not completely converted to "our way of thinking" and then through the war with Iraq, focus was lost against the Taliban. Similarly, after the easy dismissal of Saddam Hussein, the questions about how to proceed next led to great tension back at home and counterinsurgency abroad. By all measures, we have had our starting step on the journey to the crisis. What about the other key common events or concepts?

The election of 2006 and 2008 clearly point to two of the things on the list: new political voices, overt/active opposition to the government. Coming out of the 2004 Presidential election, two new groups—codepink and moveon.org hit center stage. Codepink began in 2002 while moveon.org was first on the scene in 1998 during President Clinton's last years, yet both really became better known as active opposition to the governing policies of the Bush White House years. As "far left" groups, both organizations played critical roles in the 2006 midterm election victory by the Democrat Party. On the other end of the political spectrum, after the election of President Obama in 2008, the "far right" found it's new political group in the Tea Party movement. Just as in 2006, these new political activists contributed greatly to the 2010 election takeover of the House of Representatives by the Republican Party. With both the right and the left, we must continue to watch to see if these groups merely shift the ideology of a current political group, such as happened in the 1920s and 1930s, or if either might become an entirely new political party as with the emergence of the Republicans in the 1850s or the Sons of Liberty in the 1760s. Neither group has been as violent as the Sons of Liberty, but in both cases (right and left), extremists have emerged either speaking violence or taking extreme measures against the target of their ire: President Bush for the far left, President Obama for the far right. There are other groups, of course, and all of these activists, whether gathering for political meetings or writing their frustration online, are very close to overt opposition to the government. As of now, there have been no openly acknowledged plots on key leaders lives such as King Charles and his brother James faced, nor have any houses been burned like with the Sons of Liberty or jails attacked by the anti-slavery crowd. Yet, the anger against those in government is palpable.

Most of the anger felt from many Americans today is due to a sense that the governing leadership is very weak. In 2000, Republicans were generally happy with the election of President Bush. To them, they saw that election as a culmination of ending the frustration of the Presidency of Bill Clinton. Republicans controlled both houses of Congress and appeared poised to continue a move of middle-conservative set of acts. Yet, to the left in the country, Bush has stolen the election. Worse, to some, he seemed to merely be a bumbler intellectually, or at best a "good ol' boy"—great for having a drink together, but not the kind of man to lead the country. In 2008, the election of Obama was seen as the coming of an intellectual. Yet, by 2010, Democrats were among the loudest complaining that the new President had done little in office and perhaps had made things worse, especially concerning the economy. So, at a time when the country needs confident, solid leadership often seen prior to the Fourth Turnings, we find instead weak leaders. President Buchanan's failure to demonstrate any solid leadership allowed southern leaders a free hand during the lame duck session before the inauguration of Lincoln. Similarly, King James II was particularly weak in his actions, and poor political allies in Parliament undermined both him and his brother Charles. In the 1760s, King George III would go through 5 Prime Ministers in 7 years in a failed attempt to find anyone who could navigate the treacherous waters with the colonies. Then as now, the failure in leadership opens the door for new political voices as well as sending poor signals to the populace.

The weak leadership, just as we have seen in the other roads to crisis, continuously makes misguided governing decisions that indicate a growing distance between the government and the people. Whether looking at the choices in Acts like the Patriot Act (which neither President has really handled well) or responses to natural disasters (Katrina for President Bush, the Gulf oil spill for President Obama), the decisions of the governing leaders is consistently poorly received. At times, the Congress seems to choose to push through legislation that they know is against the will of the people, most recently seen in the choices of the Congress to pass a version of universal healthcare. During the last election cycle

(2010), in state after state, city after city, angry citizens came to meetings with their various representatives to yell, scream, and otherwise loudly complain about the decisions being made. The reaction by the politicians looked like actors reading a script from Prime Minister Grenville's stunned responses to the uprising in the Stamp Act. Much like Senator Stephen Douglas during the 1853-54 senatorial debates about the railroad (or his later debates in 1858 with Lincoln), who simply could not perceive the depth of the anger of the people relative to the recent decisions in the Compromise of 1850, the politicians of today seem incapable of perceiving that the distance between them and the people is now vast. Today, it is considered a normal point of view for citizens that politicians who work in the Capitol city, Washington DC, have no connection for what "real life" is like.

That's six of our eleven common traits. What about the rest? Well, we've already discussed the writings. This one will be harder to track until the actual Crisis bursts upon us. If it indeed is an environmental disaster, then *An Inconvenient Truth* could be the best possible choice, regardless of whether you think the science is correct, or fairly presented or not (Southerners didn't think Harriett Beecher Stowe had fairly shown slavery either). If the crisis is purely political, then we face a wealth of choices, which is actually part of our setting, part of our journey. I am convinced that future historians will teach their college classes that the new speed of technology and communication played a critical role in the events that transpired. In fact, the equivalent of *Common Sense* may not be a book at all; it could simply be the emergence of Twitter or the smart phone. Maybe it will be a TV show like Jon Stewart's *The Daily Show*. In any case, we have too many choices with too many talking heads (all of them paid entertainers it bears noting), who are striving to have the greatest impact on us. In the end, like Paine and Stowe, and yes, even Hitler to some degree, the person who plays this role might be largely unknown before the publication of this important work.

Speaking of communication speed leads us to see how the new instant access of the Internet has completely transformed information exchange. First there was simply the presence of bloggers who could and did move faster than more traditional media. Alongside them came web 2.0 type websites that allowed more user interaction and control. Digital became commonplace within the world of images and with the arrival of the "flipcam" in 2009, tied to sites like youtube.com, photojournalists became "everyman." Status updates from facebook and twitter increased the sense of interaction that occurs between people, and the new "mini-computers" (typically called "smart phones" though they really are computers) allowed people to update from everywhere. Imagine how the Kansas-Nebraska act would have played out with people posting videos on youtube and others tweeting about events happening in real time. These "social media" darlings have unleashed a form of citizen action unknown in world history. Not only is the speed of communication unprecedented, but also the connection is global.

Economic distress? Well, in a word, yes. We have that. As I discussed in chapter two, the situation for the country economically is as bad as ever, now a full two years after President Obama's election when correction was promised. The point of having the distress is not just the economics of it all, but also the impact to the people. The citizens of London had barely gotten over the Fire and renewed Plague when the financial meltdown occurred in 1672. Meanwhile, King Charles and the leaders in Parliament seemed to live on as if nothing had really happened; they were still fine and living well. In the 1920s, when the average American family made BELOW the poverty line, the rich upper crust were living well, enjoying the fine activities of life. Like today, those average citizens had to live on credit in order to merely get by, let alone enjoy anything exciting. During the Depression itself, to try and avoid the emotional stress of the moment, many would make the nickel hotdog from the cheap seats at a baseball game their only meal. You can bet that the very wealthy of FDR's crowd were not eating hotdogs as their only meal. Today, with the average ticket price for a sporting event climbing towards triple digits and a hotdog and coke more than $10, the ever-widening disparity between the haves (the small percentage at the top) and have-nots (the growing percentage of us who find +$3.00 gasoline brutal on the budget) is reaching explosive proportions. As we saw in Germany during the late 1920s, it is during the economic crisis that the citizen soon finds radical solutions as possibilities. I think that if we went back to the 1760s and asked the average person, they would have also found the concept of "tar and feathering" to be a brutal, terrorist act. They also would have found some of the political ramblings of Sam Adams to be outside the pale and worthy of censure. Yet, when you bring in the economic crunch that many felt in those days, the radical possibility of rising against the King became a reasonable concept.

Which brings us to the last three common attributes that we uncovered: bloodshed in the streets, an event that provokes misguided government response that galvanizes the citizens, and the unforeseen trigger event that brings the onrush of events. None of these events has seemed to have hit yet, or if they have, then their presence is not fully clear. Obviously, if it were up to us, we would wish to see none of this. So far, as I write this now in April of 2011, there hasn't been any act yet that brings the war of words to actual fighting. But, three things have exploded in that possibly could be the random event. As of early 2011, there has been an explosion of citizen riots in the Middle East; one has toppled the government in Egypt and currently, Libya is in a near civil war. Meanwhile, in several states in the USA, newly elected conservative governments are attempting to enact their promises, mostly aimed at economic "belt-tightening." Of course, for government's to tighten their belt, that means less spending in some way that touches average citizens. So, in Wisconsin, Illinois, Indiana, Ohio, Florida and perhaps other states, there are large gatherings of citizens opposed to these new state government decisions. Both crises have been helped (made worse? better?) by the new technology of instant communication seen in platforms like Twitter, Youtube and facebook. Many are suggesting that the Egyptian revolution should be considered a Facebook inspired event.

We may have recently seen our "blood in the street" event. In January 2011, a Democrat Congresswoman Gabrielle Giffords was shot in Tucson, Arizona by an emotionally disturbed man, 22 year old Tucson man, Jason Loughner. Some pundits thing that Loughner targets Giffords because of her support of President Obama. Others have offered that he is connected to the Tea Party movement. Could this be our event? Compared to the previous "blood on the streets" moments like "bleeding Kansas" or the Boston Massacre, this doesn't have the size or scope.

In the end, if all things remain the same, at some point in the coming few years (I would guess between 2012-2016), some act by the government, will push someone over the line. Maybe it will be a forced vote in Wisconsin; perhaps it will be a decision that, on its face, seems innocuous at best. Few in Washington DC could really know how abolitionists or slaveholders would take the Kansas-Nebraska Act. At that point in 1854, the concept of "popular sovereignty" was only applied to lands in the far west, where few people lived. Who knew that entire college classes from the north would covenant to move west to Kansas to ensure it would be a free state? Who knew that slaveholders and abolitionists alike would attempt to use terrifying violence, just like the Sons of Liberty years before, to get their point across?

Perhaps, just like the British in 1770, the government will be merely attempting to protect certain citizens and find itself caught into a scenario where it has to open fire upon its own citizens. Maybe, just like in 1938 with *Kristallnacht* or 1932 with the Bonus Army, the government will be enforcing laws that average citizens will decide are unfair, so they fight back. In any case, as before, once that line is crossed, all things are different. No one can tell what kind of random event will trigger a rush of events. We can only hope that as we all face the events of our time, we will be ready.

Fifteen

How Do You Prepare?

On April 9 1865, Wilmer McLean, a merchant living in central Virginia, was surprised to see a Confederate solider, Colonel Charles Marshall riding towards him. McLean lived in a very small crossroads called Appomattox and the Civil War had come to him. Colonel Marshall asked McLean if he knew where General Robert E Lee could meet with Union General U. S. Grant. Reluctantly, McLean offered his own house. A few hours later, the surrender of Lee's army to Grant was complete and, for all intents and purposes, the Civil War was over.

That McLean was the local citizen whose house was used is amazing. Four years earlier, the war's first major battle had occurred near Manassas, Virginia. At that battle, McLean's lived near Bull Run creek, in the midst of what would become the battlefield; his house was thus used in 1861 as a headquarters for the Confederate army. Though a supporter of the cause of secession, as the war continued in that region of northern Virginia for another year, including another major battle in Manassas in the summer of 1862, McLean decided that he was going to move his family. So, in 1863, he moved to what he assumed was the quiet of central Virginia. Two years later, the Colonel came riding over the hill and in a whirlwind of events, the major participants of the war, Lee and Grant, were sitting in his living room. The crisis had found him despite his best efforts to escape and hide.

Is there anything you can do about everything I have written to you? McLean decided that he was going to move from battle, and by all accounts, he did accomplish that. We know that his first house was hit by cannon fire during the 1861 battle, so this desire to avoid the war was not merely a philosophical issue. He had children and wished for them to avoid any danger. Yet, in the end, the war came to him. And, there was a cost for what he went through, even at the end. Many of the men who accompanied Lee and Grant realized the significance of the event, so they basically took all of the furniture in the parlor where the surrender was signed. They even took one of the dolls that belonged to McLean's daughter Lula.

I didn't write this book to try now to sell you on some concept of avoiding the crisis. I certainly am not going to ask you to sign up for some annual newsletter to show you how to invest in gold or special garden seeds. I have no idea what the crisis will be, or when it will even hit. Sitting here typing in 2011, it sure feels like it could come now, breaking open like a flood. Yet, even after the 1770 Boston Massacre, there were 3 silent years between that event (one of the last on the "road to crisis") and the Tea Act that sparked the final events. We cannot predict the years or dates of events to come. I am not going to tell you now to stock up on some supposedly precious item. What I am telling you though is that the event is coming. So, what can you do?

Clearly, others than myself believe bad things are going to happen. Just in the past few weeks, I have heard radio advertising to buy gold, to buy non-genetically enhanced seeds or to listen to an online recording of why the country's financial meltdown is assured. Not surprisingly, that online recording ultimately ended up asking the listener to subscribe to a newsletter for $49 a year. Some of those ideas could be useful. My wife and I have recently planted a small garden, partially in hopes of reducing our food bill somewhat, but also to remind myself of how to tend a garden. My family still owns land in East Tennessee and we won't be looking to sell it anytime soon, but we aren't planning to move there either.

Perhaps you should consider trying to spread some of your financial resources around, though if real financial meltdown happens as it did in Germany in the 1920s, it probably won't matter. Should you get a gun? Maybe, though there are many internal values questions that you and your loved ones should answer before you just casually take that approach.

As I alluded to in the previous chapter, maybe you might consider moving. Like McLean, no one really wants to live in a warzone. Will you be able to move, let alone sell your house, if a military crisis happens around us? But as I tell my students, if an enemy army is approaching your city, get out. But, if you leave, will you abandoning friends and relations who might be counting on you to participate in helping lead through the crisis?

Still, that kind of "planning" is dependent on knowing what kind of crisis we are really going to confront. We don't know. Now what? The type of thinking that I want to suggest are perhaps more philosophical, deeper. As McLean found out, you can't necessarily avoid the crisis; sometimes it will come to your door.

The first step you have already taken, at least a little. That is to know your history and the history of our country. By almost any account, the United States is one of the most successful countries in world history. Clearly, it remains an exceptional place to live if we give any credence to the millions of immigrants who continue to move here. What that tells us is that there is a set of values, a set of concepts that created our country and still attracts people today. Logically, if there is such a set, we need to know them and protect them. While we can always look for ways to do things better, and at times, we admit that everything done in the past wasn't perfect, but on the whole the concepts and values that created this country remain viable. President Obama referred to some of our old national values— "hard work and honesty, courage and fair play, tolerance and curiosity, loyalty and patriotism"— during his Inaugural Address in 2008. As he implied, we need to return to those values. Yet, how can anyone return to values if they have no idea the history of those values? This short book should only be your first step. Go read the Constitution to see what the Founders intended for government. Read about the American Revolution to learn precisely what they were fighting to achieve. Go beyond the superficial writings about the Civil War in order to understand the deeper argument about government and the Founders' desires to limit government power. At the end of the day, as I have shown you, each Great Crisis involved a change to government. As we move forward, you have a chance through voting, through active participation to have a voice, but if you don't know our history, how do you know what to vote for? How do you know you are supporting the correct side in the growing philosophical divide?

Secondly, each person must really examine his or her own personal values. What, exactly, do you believe in? Who are you? What do you stand for? When life is easy, few care about what you believe in, and perhaps in some respects, it doesn't matter. When, however, life is fragile and the world is changing around you, you had better know what you really believe in. What would you die for? Where is your integrity and what lines won't you cross? I obviously can't tell you what to believe in; as a Christian, I am confident in my faith in Jesus Christ as the Son of the one true God. He guides my life and provides instruction about what values I should hold. Yet, the internal values are not merely spiritual thoughts, but related to action during life. If the financial issue becomes more extreme, perhaps becoming "THE" crisis, we may find ourselves living in a prolonged state of being unable to buy anything. If your values reflect simple living, you will be better prepared to confront that situation. Moreover, as you connect to our historic American values, particularly the values cherished by your local community, you will be positioned as a "team player." Any others who appear completely detached from the important historic values of the community may be seen as a threat. You must be ready to know exactly what you are living for, and for what you are willing to sacrifice.

I would, however, encourage you to comprehend that Christianity was indeed a unifying foundation for our national values. Certainly I am not trying to suggest that everyone who came to our country in the founding period of 1607-1750 were practicing, devout believers. However, I would contend that everyone in that period, and at least through the 1950s, agreed to the general tenants and principles of Christianity. Those very similar ideas to what President Obama mentioned in his Inaugural Address will not reappear if the common foundation upon which everyone agreed to those values has been destroyed.

Thirdly, understand that a crisis is typically the time when you MUST sacrifice. Perhaps you will lose the financial ability to eat out every week. Maybe you'll have to give up cable/satellite TV. Perhaps, that type of entertainment will simply vanish in some crisis relative to space or communication. You might find far less at the grocery store, especially if the crisis is related to environmental concerns like water issues or the renewed grain stem rust disaster.

Remember, for five years, citizens of the Confederate States of America used paper money that became worthless by 1865. There is no promise that our concept of money or wealth will survive what we are facing; preparing to confront sacrifice relative to finances will be critical to your success if that happens. We may find that most of our expected societal services like easy access to hospitals, 911 working when we want it, food stamps, public bus transportation could vanish. Paying a price to make it through a crisis will be normal and perhaps far extended past what any of us are used to. In 2004, several massive hurricanes battered my house here in Central Florida. After each, my house lost power and water, with the longest stretch being a loss of power for six days, no water for four days and a loss internet/phone for 10 days. Over the entire 6-week period, we had eight days of no clean running water and almost 20 days with no power. Now, imagine that stretched out over 12 months rather than 1.5 months. Dealing with deprivation of some kind or another will be likely for all of us. That is why your values must be secure and perhaps even more importantly, you prepare now to avoid going through the crisis alone. Take steps now to get your financial house in order while at the same time, make the CHOICE to cut-back so that if forced to do so later, you will already be mentally prepared.

Lastly, I urge you to invest in a real community of friends to sustain you. In recent years, there has been a wealth of writing about the loss of community here in the USA. Robert Putnam's excellent book, *Bowling Alone* chronicles this loss well. I have spoken at length about this in my seminars given across the country; our country was founded on the concept of community. From Jamestown to Oregon Trail, success of the country was predicated on working together, yet for the first time in our national history, this value has been lost. Community can be defined as a group of people working together, over time, to build an atmosphere of respect, of service to others and of shared accomplishments and actions. It must be cultivated and protected; it doesn't just happen. Regardless of what kind of crisis does hit, you will need others to get through. Imagine the crisis related to a lack of food, whether through environmental issues or the deprivations of war—a community of friends sharing their resources would last longer. This includes building close connections with those you can trust and forging relationships with well-placed people. Or, to say it another way, if you head into the Crisis with few friends, or worse, several enemies (say in your neighborhood or at your work), it will be harder for you to survive easily. Think about a neighborhood after a natural disaster where societal support services can't reach you---will you have the community resources to hold together, cherishing the social contract, watching each other's property in a cohesive manner to help all survive protected? Or, do you not even know your neighbors? If there was a crisis, would anyone come to help you?

Those four steps, if you begin to prepare now, will pay huge dividends later. Understanding the history of the country will help you make it through and determine what you are ready to fight for. Strengthening your own personal values will prepare you for the challenges every crisis brings; watch any movie based around these crises (American Revolution—*The Patriot; John Adams;* The Civil War—*Cold Mountain, Ride with the Devil;* Great Depression/WW2—*Cinderella Man, Band of Brothers*; obviously with all topics, there are many others to choose from); watch and you will see that your personal values will absolutely come under fire. What exactly will you do or not do? Prepare mentally to be forced to sacrifice; you might be wise to begin now to practice more simplicity in your purchasing or eating habits. Building a community of friends around you is perhaps the most important of these three steps; knowing who you can trust when all around you is changing, perhaps being destroyed, is critical to survival.

Last thought—if there is one other thing to prepare for it is this; prepare to possibly be on the losing side of the event. Remember as I have shown you, the country was not fully united during any of our crises. Even during World War 2 and the Depression, there were differing opinions about what to do next; some people found their views to be on the losing side (ask the folks living in East Tennessee when the Federal Government simply took their land, dammed the Tennessee River and created vast lakes where previously were farms). At the end of the day, history shows us that you may discover your world completely altered; your way of thinking no longer accepted. Even if you just move away (as many Loyalists did after the Revolution), the world to where you move will not be the same. Life will be different. Get ready for it mentally before it possibly becomes a reality at some future date.

Sixteen

Why Does This Matter?

As a historian, I had noticed these patterns, but the fair question from you, the reader, could be "so what?" We certainly cannot stop the great movement of history. As noted above, there will be an event, perhaps two that seemingly is not connected to anything specific to the actual Crisis yet triggers a rush of actions that drive into the nightmare. Who can stop such a thing? However, the real point to note is that each Great Crisis has led to a change in government. In fact, the working title for the book was *Great Crisis Leads to Change in Government.* The reality is that each Great Crisis ends up with something different in government of the United States, and not always for the better,.

This fact demands that we spend a bit more time looking at the common point of detached political leadership. That single common attribute from the roads to crisis deserves more scrutiny because it could be, ultimately, the core factor upon which the issue of our future hinges. This is the real reason I wrote this book. On October 31 2008, then Senator Obama made a very clear statement when he spoke at a politically rally, saying, "We are five days away from fundamentally transforming America." While he may have just been caught up in political speak at the final days of a tough campaign, and he may have just meant the excitement of electing the first African-American as President, the core idea of the phrase stuck with me. To fundamentally change or transform anything means to bring something different at the core of the thing.

That idea of change, of a fundamentally different government, was precisely what the Whigs were thinking in 1688 as they worried about the King bringing up his son, and their future king, as a Catholic. So, they took the final steps into the Great

Crisis of that time and the Glorious Revolution was the result. Now, from our vantage point, the change that they enacted, including the English Bill of Rights and the full concept of a constitutional monarchy, was a good thing. Yet, clearly, for many in England at the time, and many in the colonies, the change was tumultuous. The early decades in the 1700s saw tens of thousands decide to leave England to move to the New World. Some came for the economic opportunity but others came to still find a new kind of freedom.

Equally true in the 1770s, a fundamental change from a monarchy, even a constitutional monarchy, to a Republic was a monumental undertaking. As we look back, of course we see positives. Yet, for many of that time, soon to be known as Loyalists or Tories, the change was a terrible thing. For them, the war and subsequent American victory only brought on economic ruin and loss. Even life for the victors, as we have seen, was less stable than we have often been taught. The first 25 years from 1775 to 1800 brought revolutions and citizen uprisings (Shays' Rebellion, the "revolution of the better sort" leading to the Constitution, Whiskey Rebellion, the Revolution of 1800, and the Essex Junto) before there was any sense of real stability. Certainly, the end product, our US Constitution and a government "of the people," was an amazing development. For one of the few times since the Roman Republic, power would lay with average people who had some degree of control over their lives. Still, you must understand that the end product was a massive CHANGE in government and in the lives of the average citizen.

Hopefully, you know of the difficult period post-Civil War in that time known as Reconstruction. Even in the north, with the economic depression of the 1870s, things were not happy, not easy after the war. And, as we noted previously, the effort to save the Union had actually altered the government. Certainly, the Southerners were making an attempt to overthrow the government, or more accurately, leaving the Union because they didn't think they could overthrow or change it. Yet, to stop the rebellion, the current government style had to change to become more aggressive, more controlling. Lincoln actually took steps that make our own Patriot Act seem tame by comparison, and his bold, probably illegal stance towards the Supreme Court is scary to contemplate. His choices, and that of his government, forced citizens to accept the central government's ability to dictate morality and decisions in areas that had always been the purview of the individual. Though he would have denied it, to save the Union, Lincoln had to create a new, stronger government and the old order was largely overthrown.

The journey to crisis in the 1930s happened in the world Lincoln had created. As we saw, the people came to adapt to the new government in 1870-1900 years, though the Founders would have been horrified. Of course, to be fair, the Founders could not have foreseen the large, national corporations that seemed to control and dominate so many lives or so much money. Perhaps they too would have suggested more democracy or at least more regulatory power held by Congress. Yet, by the 1930s, to stop the bleeding in hopes of thwarting the Depression, the people were then open to accepting a socialist style of government control that radically changed the Lincoln-styled US government. When the war came, though President Roosevelt would have denied it just like Lincoln, an even larger government that was tied into all phases of common life was empowered. If the government wasn't regulating businesses like the airline industry or the agriculture industry, they were giving money to people through acts like Social Security or unemployment assistance. Meanwhile, the government continued to expand through contracts within the military-industrial complex, or copying Hitler's Germany, building our own Interstate Highway System. If the Founders had disagreed with Lincoln's actions and the government after the civil war, they would have been stunned to see the power and reach of the new Federal Government in the 1950s and since. To put it bluntly, the government of my lifetime, especially since my adult years from the 1980s on, has more power, and controls more of our personal lives, than anything King George III dreamed of in the 1770s.

To be concerned with President Obama's pre-election statement is not just a concern about his time as President. He may have the same impact as a Prime Minister Grenville, fueling revolutionary fire in the people. Or, he may simply be our own President Buchanan, a nice man who merely held the Oval Office for four years while the tension builds. Yet, the reality is that these Great Crises are not just about the crisis itself, but also about the outcome. Authors Howe and Strauss wrote that the first turning is a high period, with "a new civic order in place." Sometimes that "new civic order" has turned out for good, as we saw with the Glorious Revolution and the American Revolution. Yet, the last two crises, while ending well in one sense (elimination of slavery in the USA and then the defeat of fascism), proved to be the undoing of the good government built by the Founders. To get through the crisis, leaders took stances, made decisions that altered the government forever. Perhaps it was not as obvious through the years between the Civil War and World War II, but clearly in the years since WW2, our government has become more intrusive and controlling. Of course, with these negative changes to government, other people and events played a role. I am not suggesting that Lincoln or FDR alone subverted the country; those 80 years between events play an important role, and the citizens make choices, both individually and corporately that impact the end product. Still, the bottom line is that a crisis will rock the country. Are we ready for that? Are you? Do you know where you would stand philosophically?

Seventeen

Could This NOT Happen?

In the latter months of 1998, a concern began to sweep the nation, and indeed the connected world, that a crisis was immanent. The issue was the possibility that computers built in the past decades were ill-prepared to confront the mathematical problem of the year starting with "20" rather than "19." This potential issue became known as "Y2K" or the "Y2K bug" and by the late fall 1999, companies and cities braced for the worst. Some experts suggested that planes could crash or hospital equipment would fail as well as more mundane problems like your microwave no longer working. Books were written about the need to prepare as some thought Y2K might be related to some end of the world scenario.

I will freely admit to stocking up on water and some canned goods, though that was about it. Living in hurricane alley Florida, having extra water and canned foods is not a dumb idea anyway. I also participated in a series of seminars to help prepare my church community for the event. In November of 1999, I hosted a community wide gathering in my neighborhood; our focus was merely to prepare for the possibility of being without power or communication for some period of time, to know who each of us was. Probably not surprisingly, only a few people came, but we made the attempt. In the end, as we all know, nothing serious happened. A few glitches here and there, but overall nothing drastic transpired. Could the same thing happen here?

As I have reviewed our history and have taught these patterns for years, I feel very strongly that we are on track for the next Great Crisis. All of the signs seem clear as we work our way into the second decade. However, I am astute enough to acknowledge that, like Y2K, nothing obvious could happen. The months and years could roll by and before we know it, we could be way past 2020 with no great crisis. Honestly, I would LOVE that. As I have told audiences before, I hope we all laugh at "poor Professor Creasman for his alarmists views." I hope that happens.

I actually believe there are more reasons than just faint hope, though, that could impact the pattern. As I noted earlier in the writing, this pattern is most clearly seen in Anglo-American history. That is true for two reasons, at least: first, prior to the 1400s, there really wasn't an "Anglo" history separate from the rest of Europe and clearly there wasn't an American history; second, the pattern is predicated on a system of beliefs relative to the individual, family concepts, childrearing ideas, private property values and other ideas that, while widely known today, were unique to England (and her descendants like the USA, Canada, modern India or Australia).

In other words, there was no obvious "pattern" of a four-cycle saeculum prior to the 1400s. Strauss and Howe do demonstrate that there are other patterns historically, and the idea of various generations do occur outside of Anglo-American history, but this clear pattern of four reoccurring generational archetypes, mixed with childrearing relationships and overlaid over a dual pattern of Great Awakening and Great Crisis, began in the post-100 Years War era. It is then that historians first find the idea of an "England" really resonating with the people of the island north of the continent. Certainly there were people living on old Albion, as the Romans knew it, but the island was as much an afterthought as anything by the great powers of Europe. Charlemagne didn't bother to even attempt a conquest, believing there was not much to reward the effort. William the Conqueror did, in fact, conquer the island, but that was in an attempt to merely grow his own holdings. Over the subsequent 200 years, the families of the powerful in old Albion and old Gaul were intertwined so that, at the death of French Charles IV, Edward III of England had the strongest claim to the French lands.

The subsequent struggle through the 1300s and into the 1400s, ending in 1453 with the French side of the family in full control of old Gaul, created the clear divide between "France" and "England." The Court in London ceased speaking French and both areas became more adamant in their self-perspective of being "an us," a collected group, a nation. For the island, there was still internal turmoil, giving rise to the first civil war among the British, the War of the Roses. That tension could be seen as the first crisis for the cycle—indeed if you review the chart in chapter four, you'll note that we start counting the years at the end of the War of the Roses (1487). That family squabble was put to rest by the victory of Henry Tudor at the Battle of Bosworth Field in 1485, and then as Henry VII, he crushed the last uprising of Yorkist loyalists at the Battle of Stoke in 1487. Henry VII then oversaw the Tudor Renaissance, as Strauss and Howe put it.

Thus, if there is a beginning to Anglo-American history, there could also be an end of that same history. Of course, no one wants to consider such things, especially if you like living in our style of life, if you enjoy our way of living and our values, but throughout history we can see that empires and nations come and go. If the actual political entity (England, for example) does not disappear, the influence and impact of a nation can certainly come and go.

Yet, even if nothing destructive happens directly to the USA, our Western life and culture could end. Currently, there is a very strong "global" perspective that is in the forefront of many people's minds and views. While it isn't clear that anyone specific is clamoring for a "One World Government," the idea of a larger united entity isn't a secret. In Europe, the idea of a political union of the European Union is popular. While initially, the EU began as an economic collective, over the past decades, in 2005, the nations of Europe were poised to push for ratification of a European Constitution. Though larger nations such as Spain and Italy voted to ratify the new governing document, the effort for unification was thrown off course when The Netherlands and France rejected the document. Both countries had been seen as fully supportive, so their votes were a surprise. Still, in 2011, there are continued calls to vote for the Constitution, and possibly see that lead to a great union within Europe.

Meanwhile in the USA, there is a growing specter of a North American Union. Unlike in Europe, there are no official documents that propose any kind of union, but the North

American Free Trade Agreement, began in 1995, raised those issues. Under President Bush, the concept of a "Super Highway" to connect all three nations came under scrutiny for various reasons. Again, the idea of a political union of the three larger nations of North America has never been openly broached, but with issues such as illegal immigration, fair trade, and drug wars, the concern is at least understandable.

This idea of larger political entities is connected to another new passion seen across the globe, but particularly acute with some living in the USA. For the first time in our history, there is rise to an "anti-nationalist" viewpoint. This viewpoint comes up mostly with the issue of illegal immigration. Someone supporting the coming of immigrants to the country will dismiss concerns about legality, claiming that these people have rights also or that the opportunity to succeed in our country should be open to anyone. Few will openly call for the end of our nation, but their logic typically runs to a conclusion that suggest that there is little need for national boundaries or even national laws. So, if the cycle of history that we have uncovered is predicated on an Anglo-American set of values and mores, and if we no longer have such a nation, then perhaps the pattern would end.

More likely to derail the pattern as it approaches the next crisis would be the loss of the Anglo-American values from the history. Instead of losing the country in total, it is more obvious that we are seeing a shift in national values. As mentioned earlier, President Obama referred to some of our old national values— "hard work and honesty, courage and fair play, tolerance and curiosity, loyalty and patriotism"—during his Inaugural Address in 2009. Yet, few of those ideas have grown in importance in the past two years. Though the country gives lip service to these concepts, again and again the evidence indicates values are in decline. The past two years since he gave the speech gives us little reason to hope that these values are being restored or celebrated.

Why would that matter? Remember that the idea of the cycle is related to childrearing. At its core, how a nation raises its children sets the stage for the coming 60-80 years. While Strauss and Howe demonstrated how the pendulum swings back and forth from being too restrictive to being too lax in childrearing, through the past 400 years, we have generally raised our children with the same basic core set of values. At no point, till the past few decades, would you really have found anyone suggesting that hard work was no longer necessary or important. The nation has had its share of "cheaters" before, but until recently, the country was in agreement that cheating was bad and that those who cheated should be punished. Now, cheaters are put on TV, made famous, and given large salaries. I could go down President Obama's list of values or include others that he didn't; yet the result would be the same. As we abandon our core values, the values upon which the country was founded, children being raised into that culture will not know nor hold these historic beliefs. Thus, it is possible that the same events that previously led to a Great Crisis might only lead to confusion, consternation or perhaps, merely to ambivalence.

Why are our national values is disrepair at this moment? The easiest answer is that over the past 20-30 years, we have moved philosophically into postmodernism. Realize that the topic of "postmodernism" has led to several books much longer than this one, so I have no intention of trying to give it depth here. The simplest way to understand postmodernism is the concept that "nothing is real." Postmodernism emerged mostly through literature studies in the post-World War 2 period, and those scholars began to postulate that the words as written by the author may not exactly mean what you, the reader, think they mean. The author could use words to confuse or contradict. At the same time, so suggest the theorists, the words are interpreted by the reader, so that no matter what the author meant, the reader creates his/her own reality. I think you can see how easy it is to jump from that view to suggest that nothing is real. Nothing has value. Everything is fluid, temporary. The postmodernist talks about "hyperreal." Only the hyperreal is real, yet the hyperreal is fake.

Clearly, then, if nothing is real, then it is equally apparent that nothing is true. If nothing is true, postmodernists would argue, then how can anyone claim to present something like "core values?" Not only is the country postmodern, but also it is post-Christian. The polls will, of course, still show about 70-80% of the country claiming to be Christian, but to look around at our nation, our cities and our culture, is to debase that idea immediately. Moreover, in the past 20 years, citizens have become more open about supporting alternative religions such as Islam, Hinduism or even just outright atheism. While there is nothing wrong necessarily with someone holding a different faith view, doing so highlights the loss of the sense of a unified country as it confronts crisis. So, if there are no truths, if the majority of citizens live their lives as if nothing is true and the country has largely abandoned its Christian roots, that which unified our value system, then it is fair to suggest that the values that created an "Anglo-American culture" are gone. If there is no such culture anymore, then there is no reason to believe the historical cycle will happen as before.

Lastly, I think we have seen a sharp increase in the speed of our world in the past decade. This has happened through the explosion of communication tools, predominantly the computer. Now that we have created the mini-computer (the so-called "smart phone"), many people are mobile in all of their computing. How this will impact our world is, as of yet, not clear. Perhaps the Democracy that everyone really clamors for will emerge when the government decides to issue everyone a smart phone so that they can vote on issues as required. Many are calling the Middle Eastern revolts the "Facebook Revolution" or "Twitter Revoltuion" because the successful overthrow of regimes in places like Egypt and Tunisia were aided by social media and the ability to quickly send news, videos and pictures to the world. Maybe the *Minority Report* vision of shopping where computer screens can perform instant retina scans to properly access databases (probably run by Google) in order to show you exactly what you should go buy. How long will it be before we each can send or receive 3d holograph messages just like Princess Leia via R2D2 in *Star Wars*?

As it relates to our cycle, it is possible that the speed of communication and sense of "closeness" that we feel in the world, somehow impacts how people respond to events. Maybe had there been Twitter, King George III could have calmed the fears of the majority so that they would have found Sam Adams for him and ended the rebellion. Maybe if enough people saw a speech by a future Adolf Hitler, public pressure via facebook would be enough to ruin that person's chances at election.

On the other hand. . . .

It is possible that all of these things: speed of global communication, postmodernism, declining national values, the end of "nationalism" or the rise of larger political entities, could make matters worse. I don't mean that they could make the Great Crisis somehow bigger or more explosive. Whatever we are facing will feel just as huge as the Glorious Revolution or the Civil War did to those citizens. The citizens experiencing previous Great Crisis moments would claim that their time was as explosive, as tense, or as big as ours.

Where those modern concepts could exacerbate the situation would be in the end result. If few citizens think we should have national boundaries or national laws, then maybe they will be unwilling to fight to preserve that nation. Already, there are many citizens of the US who think the country is the "bad guy" in the current story of the world, so they seem to wish for the country to get "punished."

The change in values is perhaps easiest to see how it would impact. If few people hold to the old values, then perhaps none of them will be willing to sacrifice to preserve the nation (or sacrifice to create the new rebellion). In other words, as the possibility of a new Valley Forge emerges, or the need for a new generation to storm the beaches at Normandy, it is possible that the bulk of the citizens merely shrug and say "no thanks." Maybe as some states secede from the nation, other citizens will simply think "good riddance" and not hold any common American value that would lead to their participation in trying to fight to defend the Republic or free the slaves.

The speed in communication could perhaps make events more toxic. Add to that the issue of our mass media and how they have largely failed to take serious the purpose of journalism. Most networks are clearly aimed at making money, so the more they can inflame a story, the better it is for them. Rather than reporting information in a way that could help us navigate through an issue, we may discover that the networks, blogs and mass media merely serve to inflame passions in order to keep ratings high.

More critically, the explosion of technology has changed many of the assumed rules. This fact could end up being a good thing, I freely admit. The supporters of Democracy believe only positive impact from the "open source" world fed by immediate Twitter access. However, as author Evgeny Morozov wrote recently in *Wired Magazine,* "There's a special irony when [former] Google CEO Eric Schmidt suggests—as he did in a speech to the Council on Foreign Relations last November—that China's government will find it impossible to censor "a billion phones that are trying to express themselves." Schmidt is rich because his company sells precisely targeted ads against hundreds of millions of search requests per day. If Google can zero in like that, so can China's censors." The scary reality of the technology is, just as George Orwell predicted, that technology could be used against us.

At the end of the day, I'm not sure how these very current issues will impact the story. I think they could have a great impact. Maybe they will forestall the event; perhaps they will speed its coming (remember, we could be IN the Great Crisis now as I write this in early 2011). Postmodernism poses the greatest possibility to reshaping or breaking the cycle. As we move through this decade, we will see what we see. By 2020, I think we will know.

Eighteen

What now?

Do you remember Doc Brown's Delorean? Ted and Bill's magic phone booth? Let's play a game of imagination as we end this book. Marty McFly explodes onto the scene outside your house and invites you to hop in. In a flash, he hits 88 mph and, bam, the next thing you know everything around you changes. When you ask him where you are, he merely points to the time scope on the dashboard and you see its 1858? Or maybe it says 1773? What would you do?

OK, sure, it's a silly game of imagination, and unless Marty didn't bring enough plutonium, you'd demand he take you back to your own time. Me too! But, what if, like in all three of those movies, you couldn't just easily get back? What if, after he dropped you off, he disappeared? Then what?

Let's make it easy—you are in Virginia in 1858. Do you march to Washington to seek an audience with President Buchanan? If you were forced to live there, would you end up owning slaves in order to economically feed yourself? Would you try to free slaves? Would you assist John Brown or would you try to warn the political leaders of Virginia it was coming? Or, if its 1772, do you try to reach Governor Thomas Hutchinson in Boston to warn him of the impending debacle with the tea ships? Or, since you are in Virginia, do you try to find George Washington to give him advice about the coming war?

Would you try to flee, move to the west perhaps (unless you arrived in 1928, in which case moving to the West would probably be economically the worst decision)? If you stay, the coming conflict, the coming war, will certainly surround you. What if you didn't come in Doc Brown's Delorean, but, through a typical sci-fi twist of fate, you just woke up in that time, and discovered you had a family? What then? How do you protect them?

Do you see what I am getting at? You ARE ALIVE in that same type of period, similar critical moment in history. Maybe it's not the equivalent of 1858 but more like 1852, before the railroad decision. Maybe its 1764, before the Stamp Act, but make no mistake, the evidence is that we are in that equivalent year. Here's another quick rundown of how we got here by showing you a short version of the years between crisis, that each crisis led to a new round of the four cycle period.

1689—English Bill of Rights creates the first Constitutional Monarchy; but early 1700s "Salutary Neglect" combined with America forced to defend itself in early "Colonial Wars" (circa 1720-30) **LEADS TO** the 1754 Albany Congress; Ben Franklin suggested commonwealth combines with new American "definitions" of words like representation, economics, taxes, trade, liberty, voting

SO—The American Revolution was fought about control— Rebels win, and a Republic is born

1781—the Founders create a Republic but are divided over what that really means; but 1800, Jefferson-styled focus on "the people" **LEADS TO** 1832, Jacksonian "Democracy," and his own, new "definitions" about government, the Presidency itself, creating a more powerful American Presidency

SO—The Civil War was fought about states and citizens losing local control to the federal government—Rebels lose, the Union is saved, the slaves are freed, but the government is altered, exerting more power and control.

1865—Lincoln brings in more centralized government, moving away from local focus (thus, "States' Rights" no more); but 1880 Populists focus on need for more Democracy PLUS more Government **LEADS TO** 1912 Wilsonian Progressive Government with even more Federal Government oversight, more control, though with more supposed help for the little guy

SO—The Depression/WW2 fought to maintain stronger Government control against enemy of rich capitalists and dictators, both demonized to the point where citizens accept new change—Government wins, though altered in terms relative to power, economic impact and control.

1945—FDR wins unprecedented 4th term, idolized by most citizens; but 1960s JKF/LBJ focus on even more government control creating economic malaise **LEADS TO** 1980s Reagan Revolution, supposedly a return to conservative governing principles *of the Founders;* true to some effect, but "Big government" remains entrenched even with Republicans in office seen in new cabinet positions, war on drugs, expanded military spending, continued (increased??) earmark/pork barrel spending into 21st century

SO—new Great Crisis period . . . .

In the last decade, as we have discussed, we are involved in a War on Terror with military troops literally around the globe. We are under a more watchful government with The Patriot Act, Homeland Security and the TSA as examples. We elected the most openly Socialist President pushing for more government control and a desire to "fundamentally transform" the country. We are now seeing aggressive, angry political groups like moveon.org and the Tea Party; will there be more rebels? Is there a Sam Adams, a John Brown, a Milo Reno to enflame the masses?

Since the Bush Presidency, there have been active secessionists groups in over 25 states in the Union; many remain active today. Will the government make some decision in the coming years that leads a state like Texas or California to secede? Realize that California, if it were a separate nation, would have one of the world's largest economies, at least until recently. Texas would be bigger in land size than most of the nations of Europe.

Perhaps our economic woes will reach such a situation that China, or an alliance of Middle Eastern nations, believes that can attempt to coerce some action from the country. Would such an act be an external event that unites everyone into accepting massive new change? Worse, is our moral fiber so thin that we would simply capitulate to the demands?

No one can know for sure. And, I could be wrong. In fact, as I tell groups when I speak about this, for the sake of my children, I hope I am wrong. I hope 2020 arrives and we all just laugh at my thoughts, at this book. I hope that the country recovers economically this year and we all enjoy a new level of prosperity where poverty is almost banished.

I hope that. . .but I am not counting on it.

Nineteen

Epilogue

After King James II was deposed from the throne in London, having thrown the Great Seal into the Thames River, his family lived in Versailles under the protection of Louis XIV of France. Thirteen years later, in 1701, James passed away and his son, the infamous "water pan baby" that we spoke about in Chapter Five, became the claimant to the throne, the defender of the Stuart family claims. James III, as he was known in France, attempted invasion of England in 1708 and again in 1715, successfully landing in Scotland, the site of the old Stuart family lands. He was unsuccessful both times. James III also had a son, Charles Edward Stuart, and after the failed invasion in 1715, hopes for any return of the "legitimate" king of England turned to Charles. Known more popularly as "Bonnie Prince Charlie," he was raised in Rome with a constant storyline that he was the rightful heir to the throne of England.

In 1745, some 57 years after William of Orange had first sailed from The Netherlands to invade England, Charles landed in Scotland, largely alone. In those 57 years, the old Scottish clans had not grown any more pleased with English domination leading many clans and Scots to flock to his banner. Through the fall, Charles was militarily successful, capturing the city of Edinburgh and winning several small battles, while at the same time politically garnering more support. Unfortunately, the British government was not about to allow Charles to merely march south to London, so on April 1746, a larger British army defeated Charles' army at the Battle of Culloden. Charles evaded capture and was able to make his way home, living his remaining days in exile. The cause to restore the Stuarts was finally, fully, dead.

Yet, in reality, there was never much of a cause. Certainly the "losing" side in the Glorious Revolution, political "Tories" as they were known in the decades after William's conquest, might have enjoyed the legitimate line of Stuarts restored. Yet, they did not make any real efforts to support either James III or Bonnie Prince Charlie. Many remained concerned that both Stuart leaders remained Catholic, but more English leaders were ambivalent because everyone could tell the efforts had no prospect of success.

Thus, though James II, James III and Charles Edward all wished to see the hands of time turned back, it was not going to happen. The Great Crisis had come. The Glorious Revolution was fact. There was no going back. Regardless of how one really felt about Parliament being fully in charge in England, the issue of control was no longer in dispute.

This is the reality of what a Great Crisis brings: total change from the previous. Anyone alive in the 1950s could tell that the country was radically changed from 1929, when the Great Crisis began. Some wished to go back, to end New Deal programs, afraid of the military-industrial complex, but there was no going back.

Unless something unusual takes place changing the pattern, we are going to go through our own Great Crisis. We are clearly in the fourth phase. Though, as I have said before, as participants we can't tell precisely where we are, it seems that the invasion of Iraq and contentious election in 2004 would indicate a move into the Great Crisis. Interestingly, that would be 75 years from the start of the last Crisis in 1929.

Strauss and Howe predicted that the year 2005 would be the start of the crisis phase; as you can see in the chart on the following page, 2005 would cover the 21 years of a phase of life from the end of the last phase in 1984. A child born in 1984 would be entering the "young adulthood" period, moving into a new phase of life, part of how Strauss & Howe explain the movement of generations through the saeculum. If we move 80 years from the 1929 start year of the previous Crisis, we find the date to be 2009, so the year after President Obama's election when the emergence of the Tea Party opposition first took center-stage.

Civil War Age 1788-1868 (80 years)	Jeffersonian America	Second Great Awakening 1822-1844	1831 (90 yrs to previous high point)	Rise of Sectionalism & Division	Civil War 1855-1869	1863 (83 years to previous high point)
Great Power Age 1868-1948 (80 years)	Gilded Age	Third Great Awakening 1890-1908	1906 (75 yrs to previous high point)	WW 1 & Progressive Movement	Great Depression & World War 2 1929-1948	1943 (80 years to previous high point)
Millennial Age 1948-20??	American High	Fourth Great Awakening Consciousness Revolution 1964-1984	1974 (68 yrs to previous high point)	Culture Conflict	???? Crisis 75 yrs from previous 2004 80 yrs=2009	70 yrs from previous 2012 75 yrs=2017 80 yrs=2022

I hope you are ready. As we have seen, many of the predictor attributes have already hit. Based on that, we might even construct an earlier start of the "Road to Crisis" by looking at 9/11 or maybe even President Clinton's last years. I don't think that is correct; rather I think one of the impacts of the increased speed due to technology (that change to the world that I wrote about previously) is that things like a "road to crisis" will be much shorter than we've seen previously.

Of course, the reality is that we will have to see what, precisely, the actual Crisis is before we'll know for sure. In Strauss and Howe's excellent book *The Fourth Turning*, they predicted possible demands for a new Constitution, a possible nuclear threat from terrorists, economic panic, some pandemic that destroys life, urban militia styled warfare or a war with a rogue state. They wrote those possibilities in 1997 and now in 2011, any of those possible outcomes looks likely.

If any one of those things happened, then maybe we'll note a growing conflict internationally that built over the next 3-7 years and we'll see the steps towards that event. If the crisis is something domestic (economic chaos, food or water shortage, civil rioting, new round of secessions), we'll be able to track decisions made based on that event.

For now, what you know is that there is a 500+ year old pattern that always leads to a Great Crisis, the idea of the saeculum that Strauss and Howe first wrote about. Now, though, more, you understand that once the fourth turning occurs into the crisis phase, there remains the final move into the actual Great Crisis. Through all four Anglo-American cycles, those "roads to crisis" have left us clues, another pattern to follow. In that pattern, we are able to discern common attributes, and of those 12 common attributes or concepts, we have matched a high number of them. Does that mean the Great Crisis will start in a year or so? No. We can't say that. But, based on the previous roads to crisis, we can say that there usually is no great gap as the issues move forward. Tension seems to rise. The philosophical divide increases. Both sides of the issue grow increasingly fraught with worry that their "way of life" or "viewpoint" will be marginalized or removed completely. They become willing to "fight" for their view, either to change or defend status quo. At that point, we simply need the final trigger, often an event that is shocking that then forces the hand of the government to respond and that response, as we noted, brings an open and outward response.

Knowledge is power. Now you know. Take advantage of the knowledge.

About the Author

Carl Creasman has been speaking professionally for over 25 years to a wide variety of audiences here in the United States and abroad in such diverse places as Haiti and England. A gifted communicator, one College President stated, "Carl has a gift for making complex ideas easily understood," reaching audiences "with a style and message that transcends the cultural challenges of postmodernism." A speaker for numerous colleges, churches and professional organizations, he urges his listeners to achieve excellence in their personal, educational, and professional lives.

Carl began speaking during college at Auburn University, and continued to do so while earning two Master's Degrees, one a Master's of History and the other a Master's of Divinity. Throughout his adult life, Carl has combined his ability as a communicator with his love of working with people. He has worked in diverse arenas such as coaching an Olympic training swim team, working construction for a custom homebuilder and ministering as the Student Pastor of a local church.

Currently both the Senior Pastor at an innovative young church, Numinous Inc, and a Professor of History at Valencia College in Orlando, FL, he is known for his inspiring presentations and his concern for his students. At Valencia, his student reviews tell a consistent story of value as reflected by a common statement—"you are one of the best teachers I have ever had; thank you for changing my life."

Carl is married to Kim, recently celebrating 22 years of bliss together. They have three lovely daughters, Logan, Meryn and Brynn. Since 1993, they have lived in Winter Park, FL, moving from Wake Forest, NC where Carl completed his seminary degree.

As a Professor, Minister and Speaker, Carl mixes history and spiritual depth with motivational, value-laden stories to drive home a passionate message that will leave your participants "inspired, encouraged and ready to charge forward into life." Or, as one recent participant stated, "Your words have inspired me to take a deep leap of faith and change my young life for the better."

"Carl Creasman will bring a word and story to students that will ring with authenticity . . .and plant seeds of transformation in their thinking. And believe me, Carl can bring it."
Ken Dillard, University of Cincinnati, Instructor in Leadership Development

"Carl Creasman is an innovative speaker. Students relate well to the ideas, presentation, and realization of all that Carl offers."
Amy Boyer, College of Holy Cross

"Your presentation on 'Extreme Living Extreme Valor' drove home a message that was critical to the times we are living in. As you spoke to the audience about integrity, honor, & honesty, you could feel the emotion in the crowd as they took it in."
Michael Cowles, SkillsUSA Ohio Director

"Your words were inspirational, humorous and timely."
Dr. James T. King, Vice Chancellor Tennessee Board of Regents

"You have a special talent to inspire, motivate and excite others toward being the very best they can be."
Dr. Kermit Carter, Dean for Student Affairs, Calhoun Community College, Decatur, AL

"Excellent presentation; very timely for our members who work with students."
Frances Ash, Association of Florida Colleges, Region II Director

"Carl's ability to relate to students and professionals alike makes his work extremely relevant to both audiences."
Victor Felts, South-Eastern IFC Executive Director

To invite Carl Creasman to speak at your school, conference, or church, contact:

Carl E. Creasman, Jr.
P.O. Box 2031
Winter Park, FL 32790-2031
407.949.4171 or creasman@mac.com

www.carlcreasman.com